WORLD WAR II
RHODE ISLAND

WORLD WAR II
RHODE ISLAND

CHRISTIAN MCBURNEY, BRIAN L. WALLIN,
PATRICK T. CONLEY, JOHN W. KENNEDY
AND MAUREEN A. TAYLOR

THE
History
PRESS

Published by The History Press
Charleston, SC
www.historypress.net

Cover images courtesy of FDR Library; Naval History and Heritage Command; and Halsey C. Herreshoff and the Herreshoff Marine Museum. Insignias on the back cover courtesy of Naval History and Heritage Command.

First published 2017

Manufactured in the United States

ISBN 9781467136907

Library of Congress Control Number: 2016961716

Notice: The information in this book is true and complete to the best of our knowledge. It is offered without guarantee on the part of the authors or The History Press. The authors and The History Press disclaim all liability in connection with the use of this book.

Contents

Acknowledgements   7
Preface, by Christian McBurney and Brian L. Wallin   9

1. Pearl Harbor Attack Panics Rhode Islanders,
    by Christian McBurney   13
2. The Torpedo Station at Newport, by Brian L. Wallin   19
3. The Naval Air Station at Quonset Point and the
    Naval Auxiliary Air Fields at Charlestown and Westerly,
    by Christian McBurney   31
4. Seabees, Pontoons and Quonset Huts at Davisville,
    by Christian McBurney   47
5. The PT Boat Training Center at Melville, by Brian L. Wallin   55
6. The Growth of Naval Activity and Its Effect on
    Aquidneck Island, by John W. Kennedy   65
7. Liberty Ships and More: Civilian Workers and Manufacturers
    Bolster the War Effort, by Patrick T. Conley   77
8. Women at Work Outside the Home, by Christian McBurney   89
9. The Rise of Day Nurseries in Providence, by Maureen A. Taylor   99
10. The U.S. Army Handles Coastal Defense, by Brian L. Wallin   103
11. The Top-Secret Prisoner-of-War Camp at Fort Kearney
    in Narragansett, by Christian McBurney and Brian L. Wallin   113

12. The Special Prisoner-of-War Camps
   at Forts Getty and Wetherill in Jamestown,
      by Christian McBurney and Brian L. Wallin   127
13. The Battle of Point Judith and the Sinkings of
   Black Point and *U-853*, by Christian McBurney   137
14. Reflection, Relief and Rowdiness: Rhode Islanders
   React to the End of World War II, by Maureen A. Taylor   151

Appendix A: Location of U.S. Naval Aircraft in Rhode Island
   and Aircraft Types and Numbers—A Sampling at Various Dates   157
Appendix B: Naval Facilities in Rhode Island in World War II
   Showing Peak Personnel at Each Location   161
Bibliography   163
Index   183
About the Authors   191

Acknowledgements

Each of the authors contributes to the Rhode Island history blog The Online Review of Rhode Island History at www.smallstatebighistory.com.

We wish to thank the following for making this book possible. John Hattendorf, John W. Kennedy (before his retirement), John Pentangelo and Robert Doane of the Naval War College Museum in Newport provided many photographs and offered much useful information. Naval War College archivist Dara Baker and her staff were also very helpful. Fort Adams Museum curator Matthew Perry and Christopher Zeeman of the Coast Defense Study Group provided photographs and information related to the defenses of Narragansett Bay. Curator Donald Shannon of the National PT Boat Museum at Battleship Cove in Fall River provided photographs, and Charles B. Jones, author of *MTBSTC*, reviewed a draft of the chapter on the PT boat training center at Melville. Steven A. Walton, associate professor of history at Michigan Technological University, reviewed a draft of the chapter on the Torpedo Station. Dianne Rugh and Rosemary Enright of the Jamestown Historical Society provided photographs related to Jamestown and accompanying information. Jack Sprengel, curator of the Seabee Museum in North Kingstown, provided photographs and reviewed a draft of the chapter on the Seabees and Quonset huts. Keith Stokes, a contributing author to The Online Review of Rhode Island History, interviewed his mother, who worked at the Torpedo Station. Halsey Herreshoff made some great images from the Herreshoff Manufacturing Company available for this book.

The authors acknowledge the significant contributions to the study of the defenses of Narragansett Bay and other Rhode Island history by Walter K. Schroder, who passed away shortly before the publication of this book.

The authors thank Mary Keane and Bert Caudron for editing drafts of the book. Mary is also the copyeditor for The Online Review of Rhode Island History. This is the fifth book Bert has helped to edit for Christian McBurney.

Preface

By Christian McBurney and Brian L. Wallin

During World War II, Rhode Island was an armed camp. The U.S. Navy had some of its most important facilities in the country there. At Newport, the Naval Torpedo Station produced most of the torpedoes used by navy submarines, PT boats, destroyers and torpedo bomber aircraft. The Naval Training Station at Newport trained more than 500,000 officers and enlisted men during the war. The PT boat training center at Melville trained some 14,000 officers and enlisted men.

At Quonset Point, the U.S. Navy established the largest Naval Air Station in the Northeast. At its peak, more than 350 navy aircraft were at the station. Pilots were trained to fly on airplanes off aircraft carriers bound for the Pacific. Patrol flights were flown from Quonset to search for and destroy German submarines prowling the New England coast. At the nearby Naval Auxiliary Air Facilities at Charlestown and Westerly, pilots underwent risky radar-equipped night-fighter training.

Next to Quonset, at Davisville, more than 100,000 sailors known as Seabees were trained at the Naval Construction Training Center. Each year during the war, the Advance Base Depot next door shipped hundreds of thousands of tons of equipment to naval bases around the world. At the Advance Base Proving Ground, cutting-edge research was done on pontoons. The ubiquitous Quonset hut was designed and first manufactured at Davisville.

After suffering terribly during the Great Depression, Rhode Island contributed more than its fair share in making the United States the

This map shows the U.S. Navy facilities and U.S Army defenses of Narragansett Bay during World War II. Not shown are thirty-one mooring buoys in the East Passage for berthing warships; the naval auxiliary air fields at Charlestown and Westerly; and concrete lookouts and fire control buildings from Little Compton to Point Judith and Watch Hill and on Block Island. *Map by Tracy Dungan.*

"arsenal of democracy." In Providence, Woonsocket and other northern towns, the state's textile, precision tool, jewelry and rubber industries converted their factories to wartime products. More than twenty-six thousand Oerlikon-Gazda antiaircraft guns were manufactured in the state and assembled at Pawtucket. The state's largest employer during the war, the Walsh-Kaiser Shipyard at Field's Point in Providence, at its peak employed more than twenty-one thousand workers to build massive Liberty ships and combat transports as well as midsized warships. At Bristol, the Herreshoff Manufacturing Company constructed one hundred patrol boats, and smaller shipyards at Warren, East Greenwich and Wickford also built submarine chasers and other small boats.

Civilian workers in Rhode Island felt proud to contribute to the war effort. They included thousands of women employed in traditionally male jobs. Increasingly, these women wanted to use daycare nurseries to watch their children during work hours.

Jamestown and Narragansett were also the locations for three top-secret prisoner-of-war camps. The War Department used these camps for an extraordinary project to reeducate some 380,000 German POWs held around the country, preparing them to promote democracy and a respect for human rights in postwar Germany.

All of these valuable military facilities needed to be protected. This was done by the U.S. Army's coastal defense force, whose soldiers manned Fort Adams in Newport and other artillery emplacements on Narragansett Bay and along the state's southern coastline, from Watch Hill to Little Compton. A U.S. Army Air Force base was also located at Warwick.

While Rhode Island's formidable defenses around Narragansett Bay were never tested, the state has two notable claims when it comes to military incidents during the war. Just a few miles south of Point Judith, the last sinking of a U.S.-flagged merchant vessel by a German submarine (U-boat) happened on May 5, 1945, and a day later the U-boat that sank the vessel itself was destroyed by U.S. Navy warships, the last sinking of a U-boat in World War II.

During the war years, President Franklin D. Roosevelt and Vice President Harry S. Truman visited Rhode Island, while future presidents John F. Kennedy, Richard M. Nixon and George H.W. Bush received navy training in the state.

All told, Rhode Island's contribution to the Allied war effort was all out of proportion to its small size. Small state, big history, indeed!

1

Pearl Harbor Attack Panics Rhode Islanders

By Christian McBurney

Rhode Island already had a sizeable military and defense industry presence before the country's entry into World War II. Knowing that the nation could become embroiled in either or both of the wars in Europe and Asia that started in the late 1930s, the country and the state began to ramp up their military production and preparations. These activities made Rhode Island's residents worried that their state could be targeted for attack by enemy forces.

Still, Rhode Islanders were thrilled when on August 12, 1940, President Franklin D. Roosevelt arrived in Narragansett Bay on board the presidential yacht USS *Potomac* to see the navy's expanding military facilities. The president quickly inspected the Naval Torpedo Station facilities on Goat Island, peering through torpedo factory windows and viewing a completed torpedo. Thousands cheered him on Long Wharf. After reviewing 2,100 new naval recruits at the Naval Training Station on Coasters Harbor Island, the president then took his yacht under the recently opened Jamestown Bridge, with workboats following and sounding their whistles, in order to observe in the distance construction efforts at the new Naval Air Station at Quonset Point. Less than three hours after arriving at Newport, Roosevelt began his trip out of Narragansett Bay.

With tensions rising between Japan and the United States, it was not a complete surprise when news of the Japanese attack on Pearl Harbor swept over the radio airwaves on December 7, 1941. Still, it was a shock. Helen

President Roosevelt, in the front passenger seat, reviewing navy cadets on the grounds of the Naval Training Station at Newport on August 12, 1940, with Secretary of the Navy Frank Knox, Senator Theodore F. Green and Admiral Edward C. Kalbfus. *FDR Library*.

Clarke Grimes, listening to her wooden radio in Providence, wrote in her diary, "I guess this is it! Japanese dive bombers have attacked Honolulu!" The Pearl Harbor attack undertstandably created a climate of fear about the security of the country and state. This concern quickly morphed into fears of spies and saboteurs and recent immigrants who could be secret enemies.

The December 8, 1941 *Providence Journal* reported that the secretary of war's call for "increased precautions against sabotage in defense plants met [with] almost instantaneous compliance" in the state. "Rhode Island intensified its precautions against sabotage with swift action last night," the newspaper trumpeted, "to protect its sprawling defense workshops, key utility and transportation facilities serving them, and the waterfront where the materials of war are setting out on world-wide journeys."

The December 8 newspaper further reported on a five-hour meeting called by the state's governor, J. Howard McGrath, a Democrat from Woonsocket in his first of three wartime terms as governor. McGrath and the executive committee of the State Council of Defense took steps to mobilize the "State

Guard to protect public property." After this meeting, according to the newspaper, "Guards took up posts at the State Airport and extra patrols were assigned to waterfront points and reservoirs," and state police "set up an all-night anti-sabotage guard."

McGrath and the State Council of Defense further mandated the "immediate registration of all alien Japanese in Rhode Island." Those who failed to register would be "subject to detention." The governor also called on "employers and citizens who know of Japanese residents" to inform the police. In its December 9 edition, the *Providence Journal* reported that the "round-up of German and Italian aliens" in the state "believed to be dangerous to the safety of the nation" would be carried out by the Federal Bureau of Investigation (FBI), even though Hitler would not declare war on the United States until December 11. The next day, Providence's FBI office reported rounding up four Germans as enemy aliens.

The *Providence Journal* further reported that during the evening of December 7, "several extra buses rolled up to the [bus] station at Fountain Street, to carry sailors and marines back to Newport naval establishments and soldiers to Fort Adams. These extra buses to Newport were kept in service until after midnight, and other special buses were placed in service to take men to Quonset and the Jamestown forts." The New York, New Haven and Hartford Railroad—running trains out of Grand Central Station in New York City—added "special trains bringing hundreds of sailors on leave from Newport back from New York to Providence." The sailors would then have to make their way by bus to Newport.

With the surprise attack at Hawaii, concern arose about the possibility of Germany and Italy attempting their own surprise attack against the United States on the Eastern Seaboard. Military leaders remembered German saboteurs during World War I blowing up a massive munitions depot in New York Harbor on Black Tom Island. The explosion had the force equivalent to an earthquake measuring 5.5 on the Richter scale.

Thus, the stage was set for December 9, when at 12:45 p.m. an air raid alert was issued to military bases warning that "enemy planes" were "reported one hour from New York." Panic spread in the state. In Newport, the information was that German bombers were only a short distance away. How this was possible, when Germany had no aircraft carriers to launch bombers, was not explained. In any event, Newport's schoolchildren were sent home, off-duty policemen and firemen were called in and an emergency plan was put into effect. Off Newport, moored at buoy 7, the flagship of the U.S. Atlantic Fleet, the heavy cruiser USS *Augusta*, prepared for an attack.

Planes and other equipment at the Naval Air Station at Quonset Point are dispersed in case of a surprise enemy attack, December 9, 1941. *Naval History and Heritage Command.*

An unnamed newspaper reporter's telephone call to the Naval Air Station at Quonset Point about the alarm prompted an air raid alert to be sounded, leading to the evacuation of the 784 civilians employed at the Quonset Point facility, as well as 1,500 workers from nearby Davisville. The station's 3,740 officers and enlisted men readied themselves for an air raid.

Governor McGrath ordered the highways cleared and called out the state National Guard. Schools were dismissed in most towns and stayed closed for several days.

Within two hours, military authorities realized the alarm was a false one and issued the "all secure" signal at 2:46 p.m. The next day, the *Providence Journal* reported that an "erroneous alarm" from Mitchell Field on Long Island of the sighting of enemy planes off the East Coast had set off a series of air raid alerts in a wide area. In fact, the planes turned out to be U.S. Navy PBY Catalinas flying from Newfoundland, Canada, bound for Quonset Point.

Germany and Italy finally declared war on the United States on December 11. That day, Rear Admiral Edward C. Kalbfus, the chief of all U.S. Navy operations in Rhode Island, and General Ralph E. Haines, commander of the U.S. Army's Harbor Defenses of Narragansett Bay, met to discuss how to guard against a surprise attack by Germany and sabotage by enemy sympathizers. According to the *Newport Mercury*, "Heavy guards were posted at all vital spots in the bay area and gun and searchlight crews have taken up their positions." "Soldiers were swarming in from leave and furloughs," the newspaper added, noting that many had to cut short their holiday leaves.

Block Island, a small island thirteen miles south of the coast of the Rhode Island mainland, was particularly exposed—as was the case with all U.S. wars with European powers starting with the American Revolutionary War. It was also a useful place for U.S. military forces to maintain lookouts for the enemy. As early as December 8, 1941, William Doggett, the owner of a stone house perched on top of Beacon Hill—the highest point of Block Island—was informed by an army officer that his property had been seized for use by the army for the duration of the war. It was one of the first of many Rhode Island coastal homes that would be commandeered by the army or navy during the war years.

Block Islanders were not intimidated, despite residing on one of the most exposed islands on the country's Eastern Seaboard. On January 28, 1942, members of the State Council of Defense took a boat to the island to meet with local island leaders at the National Hotel. Warning of a possible German invasion and attempt to use the island as a "bridgehead" for an attack on the mainland, the state officials offered to evacuate all 671 islanders to the mainland. None of the locals showed any interest in the proposal. "There ain't a thing here any enemy would wantta [sic] get a hold of, so fur [sic] as I can see," said George Sheffield, the head of the island's civilian defense efforts. When alerted to the possibility of food shortages on a stranded island, Joseph Pennington retorted, "You can't dig clams in Westminster Street and you can't get lobsters in Scituate." The state's press admired the islanders' spunk, and the Rhode Island House of Representatives passed a resolution congratulating Block Islanders for their "patriotic fortitude." Representative Erich A. O'D. Taylor of Newport commented, "At last some people have been found in Rhode Island who are not afraid—a spirit I would like to see more generally distributed through the state." Meanwhile, Coast Guard personnel patrolled the seventeen miles of beaches, and army soldiers manned tall cement lookout towers on Block Island, as well as at key points on the state's southern coast, searching for enemy planes, ships and submarines.

Rhode Island was declared a "vital war zone," which meant strict security against spies and precautions against sabotage of military bases and war industries. Posters at defense workplaces warned, "Loose Lips Sink Ships." When seventeen-year-old Elisabeth Sheldon of Saunderstown obtained a permit to sail her fifteen-foot sailboat in parts of Narragansett Bay, her permit included this ominous condition: "ENEMY ALIENS ARE PROHIBITED ON BOARD."

In fact, there were only a very few supporters of Germany in Rhode Island. One was Nicholas Hansen, who was born in Newport of German parents and worked at the highly sensitive Torpedo Station in Newport. He admitted to the FBI that he was an admirer of Hitler, that he would "much rather fight for Hitler than the United States" and that he would be willing to participate in a plot to blow up the Torpedo Station. He conceded, however, at his court hearing in Providence in July 1942, that he was not intelligent enough to carry out such a plot on his own—his lack of intelligence was indicated by his unusual admissions.

In another case of suspected sabotage, on October 26, 1943, Henry Strunz—reportedly of German extraction—was arrested by the FBI after being accused of impeding production at the Walsh-Kaiser Shipyard in Providence. He was said to have stuck cigarettes in the nozzles of acetylene torches, loosened valves on acetylene gas tanks and conducted other acts to hinder the war effort.

As early as 1939, a Joseph Demurs, a civilian employee at the Torpedo Station in Newport from West Warwick, had been charged with sabotage. He was accused of mixing acid with lubricant oil in the torpedoes' propeller mechanism, "making it a dud."

Virtually all Rhode Islanders, including the few German Americans and the many Italian Americans, were fiercely loyal to the United States. Perhaps a majority of Rhode Islanders crowded around their radios to hear President Roosevelt's "Day of Infamy" speech. They were stirred by his clarion call, "With confidence in our armed forces—with the unbounding determination of our people—we will gain the inevitable triumph."

In the days after Pearl Harbor, thousands of Rhode Island young men flocked to enlistment centers to join the army, navy, air force or Coast Guard. College-age men on campuses in Providence and Kingston suddenly became a rare sight. Employees at the many defense plants in the state mentally prepared to work harder than ever before. Everyone thought about how they could contribute to the war effort. Women who had not before worked outside the home wondered if they would be called on. It was an exciting time. Rhode Islanders had another feeling, too: anxiety, for not knowing what lay in the future for themselves or their families and friends, state and country.

2

The Torpedo Station at Newport

By Brian L. Wallin

The Naval Torpedo Station in Newport was by far the most important military installation in Rhode Island during World War II. It was the country's principal site for research, development and testing of torpedoes and the site where the most torpedoes were manufactured for navy submarines, destroyers, PT boats and dive bombers. Manufacturing was done on Goat Island, testing on Gould Island and research, development and program management at Coddington Point. By 1944, the Torpedo Station had become the state's second-largest employer, with some 13,000 civilian workers (along with about 1,100 navy men and women). However, the Torpedo Station also became the center of a heated controversy over the quality and performance of American torpedo technology in the early years of the war.

Established in 1869 on Goat Island in the middle of Newport Harbor, the Torpedo Station concentrated at first on spar torpedoes and stationary mines. Slowly, as the technology developed, the Torpedo Station experimented with and produced the new self-propelled torpedoes that could be launched by ships or submarines.

In 1930, as technology continued to evolve, the Mark XIV torpedo intended for the navy's new class of advanced submarines was developed. (Navy terminology uses Roman numerals for numbering torpedoes.) By the late 1930s, the navy had also developed a torpedo that could be launched from airplanes, the Mark XIII. This weapon was smaller than ship-

Aerial view of a portion of the Naval Torpedo Station on Goat Island, showing the factory, piers and boats for recovering launched test torpedoes. *Naval War College Museum Collections.*

launched weapons and had a range of seven thousand yards and a speed of thirty knots. Mark XIIIs were also later used by PT boats, which required a smaller, lighter weapon. A new class of destroyers and light cruisers designed between the wars gave rise to the development of the Mark XV torpedo, which remained in service until the 1950s.

As the U.S. military began to strengthen its forces after war began in Europe and Asia, the Torpedo Station steadily expanded its Goat Island facilities with new construction and a growing workforce—4,800 by 1940. The navy also expanded its torpedo training school for enlisted and commissioned officers. As manufacturing operations on small Goat Island increased, more space was needed elsewhere for other functions.

In October 1942, a new Naval Torpedo Station annex at nearby Coddington Cove opened and shortly afterward became the headquarters of the navy's Central Torpedo Office. Goat Island became the manufacturing center, with research and other support functions transferred to Coddington Cove. Testing and overhaul was moved to fifty-six-acre Gould Island, located just off the east shore of Conanicut Island (Jamestown). Gould Island had been acquired by the navy in 1918 for use as storage and later as a test site for aircraft-launched torpedoes. Before World War II, a seaplane facility and other buildings were constructed on the southern tip of the island.

A six-mile-long firing range was set up along the eastern shore of Jamestown, extending north from Gould Island and passing between Prudence Island and Hope Island. A series of underwater hydrophones monitored weapon performance.

In 1942, to replace testing previously conducted from a barge, the navy built a two-story firing pier at the northern tip of Gould Island. The bottom floor contained four tubes for both surface and underwater torpedo launching. The second floor had an observation deck where the tests could be monitored. Test torpedoes were equipped with water-filled exercise heads. A compressed air charge blew the dummy heads off at the end of the run and triggered a dye marker, allowing the torpedo body to surface for recovery by a fleet of fifty small boats and several Coast Guard vessels assigned to the task.

Aerial view of Gould Island showing the firing pier for launching test torpedoes at the north end of the island, circa 1943. *Naval War College Museum Collections.*

Test torpedo fired from the Torpedo Station's firing pier on Gould Island, 1944. *Naval War College Museum Collections.*

During the war, more than sixty-five thousand test firings were conducted from the four launching tubes on the firing pier. An additional ten thousand tests were performed by other means, including air drops by seaplanes and torpedo planes from the Naval Air Station at Quonset Point. Recovery boats, sometimes aided by spotters in aircraft or a navy blimp, did their best to recover the exercise torpedoes. Still, an estimated 15 percent of them sank to the bottom of Narragansett Bay, never to be found again.

During the war, PT boats from the PT boat training center at Melville also used the firing range. PT boats were at first equipped with World War I–vintage Mark VIII torpedoes requiring tubes for firing. As the war progressed, PT boats switched to the lighter Mark XIII aircraft torpedo, and a simple roll-off launching device replaced the heavier launch tubes.

The recovery boats and the Coast Guard warned local mariners whenever a launch test was scheduled. Before the torpedo was fired, as a warning to recreational boaters and others, a red flag was hoisted from the firing pier and a whistle on the pier sounded. A 2013 article in the *Jamestown Press* noted that the whistle could not always be heard at the YMCA summer camp at the former Conanicut Park at the north end of Jamestown. "The navy ran a cable up to the camp that was connected to a light on the camp pier that flashed a warning to swimmers to leave the water," the newspaper reported.

In spite of these efforts, errant torpedoes were not uncommon. In 1937, an exercise torpedo fired from the submarine USS *Cachalot* narrowly missed a Vanderbilt yacht and churned ashore on Brenton Cove, plowing into an iron fence at the summer residence of Hamilton Fish Webster. Not long afterward, an unarmed Mark XIII torpedo in a practice aerial drop veered off course and punctured the hull of a small fishing boat off Newport, sinking it. During another test, in 1938, a torpedo fired from the barge off Gould Island came to rest onshore near Fort Adams. Occasionally, an errant torpedo fired from the Gould Island pier wound up on the shore in Jamestown. This occurred in 1944 when summer resident Mary Miner was photographed with her dog beside a huge Mark XIV with a dummy warhead resting on the beach in front of her home.

Seventeen-year-old Jack diPretoro of Providence, employed in a summer job in 1941 helping to build bomb storage bunkers on Hog Island, saw the wake of a torpedo heading north suddenly take a ninety-degree turn to the west directly at him, coming to rest near him on land. "You can imagine how I felt," diPretoro said, even though he knew the navy did not arm its practice torpedoes. (DiPretoro, after becoming an experienced combat fighter pilot in the Pacific, in April 1945 returned to fly TBF/TBM Avengers in Narragansett Bay, with his crew practicing torpedo launches.)

U.S. Navy torpedoes were propelled by compressed air and the combustion of highly volatile fuel that drove the propellers through turbines. However, this system produced a white wake of bubbles that enemy observers could follow back to the launching submarine. In 1941, the British captured a German U-boat equipped with a wakeless electric torpedo, a major improvement for submarine-launched weapons. The German device was turned over to the Torpedo Station, which developed the Mark XVIII within one year. Instead of an air flask, a lead-acid battery generated power. The Mark XVIII was easier to manufacture, but it was flawed in that its battery required regular maintenance.

Another top-secret device, the Mark XXIV homing torpedo, followed underwater noise generated by the target vessel. While smaller and slower than conventional torpedoes, the Mark XXIV worked more effectively, especially when launched by airplanes. A submarine-launched version, called the Cutie, was developed at Newport and put into use late in the war.

Rather than being launched from a torpedo tube, the Cutie "swam" out under its own power and sought its target.

In the years before America's entry into the war, a top-secret program at Newport, Project G53, resulted in the development of the Mark VI magnetic influence exploder for torpedoes. When passing beneath an enemy ship, the target's magnetic field was supposed to trigger the exploder, which in turn would set off the warhead, with the goal of breaking the keel of the target ship. The highly complex Mark VI did not, however, explode in combat conditions with the frequency it did in testing.

U.S. Navy torpedoes also tended to run deeper than programmed. The Mark XIV ran ten feet deeper than set due to a disparity in testing with a lighter-weight dummy rather than a live warhead. The magnetic exploder was also often prematurely triggered, and the contact exploder frequently failed to detonate the warhead. In addition, the Mark XIV occasionally would run in a circle, returning and striking the firing vessel. One such incident resulted in the sinking of the submarine USS *Tang* on October 24, 1944. Seventy-eight members of the crew were lost. Nine survivors, including the skipper, Lieutenant Commander Richard O'Kane, were picked up by an enemy warship and spent the remainder of the war in a prison camp in Japan.

All of these shortcomings were a result of a number of issues, not the least of which was the failure to fund proper testing. With the country wracked by the Great Depression and federal funds limited, the navy did not conduct live warhead testing against targets due to the $10,000 price tag attached to each torpedo and the expense of sinking a target vessel. Shockingly, no live-fire exercise of the magnetic exploder was ever conducted. The exploder's designers also failed to consider differences in the earth's magnetic field at various locations in the world and how it affected the torpedoes' performance. Furthermore, and mystifyingly, the service manual for the magnetic exploder was never printed and distributed to submarines and other vessels. In fact, the only copy was kept locked in a Torpedo Station safe. Additionally, submariners issued torpedoes equipped with the Mark VI exploder were forbidden to access the device for maintenance aboard their boats.

Submariners firing in combat situations in effect performed the testing that should have been conducted at the Torpedo Station, and in doing so, they sometimes put themselves in peril. Time and again, skippers maneuvered into ideal positions to launch a pattern of torpedoes against a Japanese merchant vessel or warship only to watch their target escape unharmed and the submarine crew be subjected to attacks by enemy

Recovering a test torpedo that had been fired from the Torpedo Station's Gould Island test pier, August 1943. *Naval War College Museum Collections.*

escorts using depth charges. Multiple complaints came back to the Bureau of Ordnance from the end of 1941 into 1943.

War patrol reports from U.S. Navy submarine skippers in the Pacific would carry wording such as "fired full salvo of stern tubes at ideal setup. Through periscope observed personnel on deck [of enemy ship] watching torpedo track that apparently passed under the ship. No hits." Another commander wrote, "Torpedoes ran true, merged with target screws, didn't explode."

Retired navy captain Edward L. Beach, who served aboard submarines in the Pacific, said the blame for these failures again and again fell against the submariners. In his book *Submarine!*, he cynically noted, "The desk-bound moguls in Washington and Newport, from their deep knowledge and great experience, were sure they knew the answers. Fire-control errors in the excitement of combat, or sheer lack of competent technique, could only be responsible for the misses."

It did not help to identify and address the problems with the torpedo that Admiral Ralph Christie, the commander of submarine forces in the southwest Pacific, was one of the fathers of the magnetic exploder. He flatly refused to allow skippers under him to disable the magnetic exploder. In Pearl Harbor, however, Admiral Charles Lockwood allowed boats to disable the device.

Eventually, a series of tests conducted in the Pacific pursuant to Lockwood's orders finally provided undeniable evidence of the flaws of the Mark VI and Mark XIV. Even then, it took an ultimatum from the fire-breathing chief of naval operations, Admiral Ernest King, to persuade the responsible navy officers to start fixing the torpedo problems. By the end of 1943, after almost two years of frustration, modifications were made at the Torpedo Station, and suddenly torpedoes began to sink Japanese ships in growing numbers. The modified Mark XIV torpedo alone contributed to the sinking of over four million tons of Japanese shipping during the war. Despite the problem with the torpedoes, American submariners still sank more than 1,178 merchant vessels and 214 warships—55 percent of all Japanese ships destroyed in the war.

Torpedoes dropped by aircraft also faced serious problems when used in combat early in the war. The U.S. Navy made its primary efforts to develop and test aerial torpedoes at the Torpedo Station. Unfortunately, the research and development at Gould Island failed to learn from and keep pace with the impressive advances demonstrated by Japan and Britain. Getting aerial torpedoes to perform as intended in combat conditions was even more difficult than getting torpedoes fired by submarines to work properly, as aerial torpedoes had to be dropped by airplanes into the water. The Mark XIII did not perform well in combat. In the Battle of the Coral Sea, for example, on May 7, 1942, twelve torpedo bombers, TBD Devastators, attacked the Japanese aircraft carrier *Shoho* but failed to score a single hit. (A second group of TBDs scored seven hits and sank the carrier.) At the Battle of Midway, a month later, fourteen TBDs from the USS *Hornet* and fifteen from the USS *Enterprise* attacked four Japanese aircraft carriers but failed to score a single hit with their Mark XIII torpedoes. Following them, twelve more TBDs from the USS *Yorktown* also failed to score a hit. Of the forty-one TBDs, a slow and plodding plane that required pilots to drop torpedoes from no higher than eighty feet, only six returned. It was an unmitigated disaster. It took Dauntless SBD dive bombers dropping bombs (and not torpedoes) to sink the Japanese carriers, leading to the first decisive and greatest U.S. Navy victory of the Pacific war.

The Mark XIII aerial torpedo underwent exhaustive testing in Narragansett Bay from 1941 to 1945, with a total of 4,500 test drops performed. Significant

A Grumman TBF Avenger launches a Mark XIII torpedo in a wartime test in Narragansett Bay. *Naval War College Museum Collections.*

improvements were made to the Mark XIII in 1943. In addition, Grumman's TBF and TBM Avengers that came into use in early 1943 were superior to the TBDs. But by that time, most of the key naval engagements in the Pacific theater had been fought. Still, TBF/TBM Avengers dropping Mark XIII torpedoes played their role in degrading and finally finishing off Japanese naval power, including sinking an aircraft carrier in June 1944.

By 1944, the Torpedo Station had become the second-largest employer in Rhode Island, with nearly thirteen thousand workers employed around the clock, seven days a week. (Only the Walsh-Kaiser Shipyard on Field's Point in Providence had more employees.) As was the case prior to the war, for security purposes, Goat Island workers were issued identification cards and transported by a navy ferry from Government Pier in downtown Newport. Navy employment proved a special boon for residents of Jamestown. Some

20 percent of the island's population worked for the navy, many of them at the Torpedo Station, requiring them to commute by ferry across to Newport before taking the brief ferry ride from Government Pier to Goat Island.

Another serious issue faced by the navy in the first few years of the war was a shortage of torpedoes. This could be traced in part to the deeply entrenched union presence at Newport. Many employees worked their entire adult lives at Newport, and jobs were often passed down from father to son. Navy administrators at Newport found it almost impossible to fire an employee because of the influence of the unions, which were also supported by state politicians, including U.S. senator Theodore F. Green.

At Newport, building a torpedo was comparable to handcrafting a Swiss watch. Work done in the highly controlled union environment focused on individual, rather than assembly line, operations. In a 1990s interview with author Robert Gannon, machinist Fred Scheibl, who worked at the torpedo factory for forty-three years, explained that each part was custom made by individual workers who each kept his own meticulous, detailed specification records in a "butcher book," which was a notebook made of meat-wrapping paper. "When we changed something, we'd note it there, rather than document it," he said. It was an art, and in many cases no two workers did the most delicate jobs in precisely the same way. Manufacture of a stock of replacement parts was also frowned on, often forcing navy crewmen to cannibalize parts from other torpedoes.

Until 1942, Newport turned out only one or two torpedoes a day, despite having three shifts of workers. After Pearl Harbor, demand for torpedoes quickly outstripped production capabilities. By 1942, 1,442 torpedoes had already been used and the navy was running out of "tin fish." Production was increased only by hiring more workers. To address the shortfall, additional manufacturing was established, using assembly line operations for some aspects, in Alexandria, Virginia; Keyport, Washington; and Forest Park, Illinois. However, as Rhode Island historian Maury Klein noted, assembly line operations to produce the control gear that kept the torpedo on target and beneath the water was exceedingly difficult. He wrote, "The mechanical artists at the Newport Torpedo Station…crafted this complex mechanism lovingly by hand, with no two parts interchangeable. It took them fifteen hours to assemble one unit." The Bureau of Ordnance asked Westinghouse to mass produce them, but it could not do it during the war.

In an effort begun in 1941 to help beef up employment to meet production demands, students from Newport's Rogers High School participated in a vocational program that eventually led to many of them being hired

An errant test Mark XIV torpedo launched from the Gould Island firing pier ended up on the coast of Jamestown near the house of Mary Miner in 1944. *Jamestown Historical Society.*

at the Torpedo Station. By late 1943, 2,598 students had completed the program; the classes ended in December 1944.

Ruth Barclay Stokes, raised in the North End of Newport on Vernon Avenue, recalled that her older sister, Delores, in late 1942 was one of the first women of color to complete a two-month machinist training course and be hired as a machinist at the Torpedo Station at Goat Island. After graduating from Rogers High School in May 1941, Ruth started nursing school, but she later decided to serve her country by joining her sister working at the Torpedo Station. She recalled that most of the thousands of employees were women, and they included many of her classmates. She was not a union member and did not recall being discriminated against on account of her Native American and African American heritage, adding that "everyone was focused on contributing to the war effort...[and] morale was high since many of the women had husbands, brothers and fathers fighting overseas." She least liked the daily ferry rides to and from Goat Island, "particularly in bad weather."

Eventually, the Torpedo Station at Newport produced some 13,000 Mark XIVs for the war effort, out of a U.S. total of 14,881. Submarines fired 6,852 of the Mark XIVs. Overall, some 50,000 torpedoes of all types were produced by all manufacturers.

Almost immediately after the war, manufacturing at Goat Island was downsized; by the end of 1945, employment had been reduced to about nine thousand workers. Torpedo production ended at Goat Island in 1951, and the manufacture of torpedoes was contracted to private defense companies. That same year, the U.S. Naval Torpedo Station was reorganized as the Naval Underwater Ordnance Station, and all activities were centered at Coddington Cove as part of the Naval Underwater Systems Center, which continues its underwater warfare mission today.

The navy declared Goat Island surplus in 1960. As part of the island's private development, a causeway was built to the mainland, and a large marina and hotel complex were constructed, turning the island into a popular tourist and yachting center. Only one Torpedo Station building remains: the yard craft office built in 1941 to serve small boats. Located on the east side of the island, it houses a restaurant and recreational marina.

Today, some 70 percent of Gould Island's fifty-six acres is a nature preserve under control of the State of Rhode Island. The navy retains title to the northern seventeen acres, where most of the buildings had been torn down by 2001. The powerhouse smokestack and a portion of the firing pier remain as prominent landmarks. The Naval War College Museum at Newport contains a display highlighting Newport's role in torpedo development. A smaller display is exhibited at Fort Adams. The Torpedo Station lasted less than a century, but it made an indelible mark on the evolution of modern warfare.

The Naval Air Station at Quonset Point and the Naval Auxiliary Air Fields at Charlestown and Westerly

By Christian McBurney

The Naval Air Station at Quonset Point was the largest navy air base in the Northeast during the war. Next door in Davisville was another massive U.S. Navy facility, the Advance Base Depot. With their deep-water ports, both facilities were visited by even the largest U.S. Navy warships, including aircraft carriers, and the largest merchant vessels, including Liberty ships. During the war, in 1943, new auxiliary—but still substantial—airfields were established at Charlestown and Westerly. The development of these impressive military facilities from virtually nothing is a wonderful tale.

In the late 1930s, as war approached in Europe, and Japan's intentions in China and the Pacific appeared increasingly ominous, the United States reluctantly turned its attention to military preparedness. Despite the isolationist sentiment within the country at large, President Franklin D. Roosevelt in 1937 pushed to bolster the naval forces. In turn, Congress authorized funds to increase the size of the U.S. Navy.

The U.S. Navy at the start of 1938 had only one thousand planes, but due to efforts at military preparedness, that number leapfrogged to fifteen thousand by July of that year. Realizing that this number of aircraft could not be supported by existing airplane bases, Secretary of the Navy Charles Edison created the Hepburn Board to advise on air base expansion. William Slater Allen, then chairman of the Rhode Island Industrial Commission, claimed he first brought Quonset Point to the attention of the Hepburn Board. In its December 27, 1938 report, the Hepburn Board rated Quonset Point "the most favorable site" in the New England–Long Island area. This decision was met with some opposition among congressmen representing eastern states, who hoped their respective state would be the location of a large air station. The controversy ended when Quonset Point was inspected by the House Naval Affairs Committee in 1939. Tucked away in relative safety up Narragansett Bay, it was centrally located to protect New England, Long Island and New York City. With some dredging, Quonset Point could serve as a deep-water port for even the navy's largest ships. It would also benefit from being next to Newport's navy facilities, as well as close to navy bases in Boston and New York City.

Hoping to spur the federal government to act, the Rhode Island General Assembly agreed to transfer land that was a former National Guard camp to the federal government on April 5, 1939. Most of the land in the Quonset area was rolling land with woods, swamps and sand, but it also included some six hundred summer cottages and several large farms, including the Romano Vineyard, which had gained a reputation for producing communion wines during the Prohibition era. Roosevelt signed the appropriation for $1 million for land acquisition in May 1939.

The navy first constructed seaplane hangars and ramps at Quonset. Starting in September 1939, more than two years before the United States entered the war, these facilities supported PBY Catalina seaplanes on Neutrality Patrol flights, searching for foreign submarine activity in Rhode Island Sound and Long Island Sound.

In Washington, D.C., Rhode Island's two senators, Peter G. Gerry of Newport and Roosevelt's New Deal ally Theodore F. Green (both of whom were on the Naval Affairs Committee), went to work to support bills to fund the effort at Quonset. In May 1940, $24,204,000 was asked of Congress by the navy to finance the project.

The U.S. Navy Department awarded the construction contract to the George A. Fuller Company of New York, bypassing a local Rhode Island firm that both Roosevelt and Green favored. The Fuller Company did promise to subcontract to Rhode Island manufacturers and wholesalers when possible. (Gilbane Building Company of Providence became one of the subcontractors.)

Fuller was one of the largest construction contractors in the United States, having led the construction of the Lincoln Memorial (1918) and the U.S. Supreme Court Building (1933) in Washington, D.C. The Merritt-

Chapman and Scott Corporation, headquartered in New York City, was also awarded parts of the Quonset construction contract. Albert Kahn Associates, the modernist industrial architect for Detroit's automakers, designed the seaplane hangars and many other buildings at Quonset.

Construction of the base was an amazing accomplishment. As the largest air station in the Northeast, it was expected to take two years or more to complete. But workers finished the job in one year. Said one U.S. Navy officer, "The spirit of cooperation between the contractors and the Navy won the battle for time."

Construction started on July 16, 1940, with a massive fill project. A total of 12 million cubic yards of mud from the bay filled 400 acres of land behind two miles of bulkheads driven into to the bay and turned a triangular land mass that jutted into the bay into a square one—to provide runways for land-based planes. Taking that reclaimed land into account, and including Hope Island (on which bomb storage bunkers were constructed), the naval air base would be built on about 1,256 acres. Some eleven thousand men and women, most of them Rhode Islanders and many desperate for employment, worked on the project.

The first Quonset Point contract included 20 million cubic yards of dredging and the construction of an 80- by 1,170-foot carrier pier, four landplane hangars, two seaplane hangars, concrete runways, barracks for 1,680 men, an assembly and repair shop, a three-story general storehouse, an aircraft storehouse, underground potable water storage and storage for one million gallons of aviation fuel. Eventually, more barracks were built to house a total of 15,000 personnel and fuel storage capacity increased to almost three million gallons. The unusually high water table and predominantly sandy nature of the soil at Quonset Point led to construction difficulties. Quicksand deposits were even found at three places, one of which had to be worked on to permit fuel storage there.

At the navy's commissioning of its new facility at Quonset on July 12, 1941, radio announcer Fred Friendly, then just twenty-five years old and beginning his brilliant media career, described Quonset as "Boomtown, Rhode Island," and waxed enthusiastically:

> *Enough asphalt runways to build a two-lane road from here to Boston. A sewerage plant almost large enough to serve the city of Westerly. Enough dormitories to house the entire student body of Brown and Rhode Island State College and Providence College combined. Enough telephone wires to run a line from here to California. A cafeteria large enough and efficient*

Dedication ceremony for Naval Air Station Quonset Point, July 12, 1941. *Naval History and Heritage Command.*

enough to fill 2,000 sailors' stomachs in less than an hour. Indeed Quonset, USA is a great city.

This is a democracy in action, for you who claim democracy is slow. Here at Quonset is a melting pot of O'Neils, Murphys, Gustafasons and Jones and Kohns and Marinos. America's melting pot. All religions, a city being built in less than a year....Yes, a magnificent city to guard our Nation's cities. Quonset, USA. This is America at her very best.

At the commissioning ceremony, a number of U.S. Navy luminaries spoke, including Rear Admiral Ben Moreell, chief of the Bureau of Yards and Docks, and Commander A.C. McFall, the first commanding officer of what officially was called Naval Air Station Quonset Point (or NAS Quonset Point).

In March 1942, the U.S. Navy also established its first Advance Base Depot, locating it north of Quonset Point at neighboring Davisville. From the original 85-acre tract, the base was expanded to cover a total of 1,892 acres. Twenty miles of railroad and forty miles of road were constructed; a

Aerial view of the massive facilities at the naval air station at Quonset Point, highlighting its four runways, circa 1944. *Naval War College Museum Collections.*

pier, 1,200 feet long and 250 feet wide, capable of berthing four ships, was built; and a channel, 3,000 feet long and 1,500 feet wide, was dredged to give access to deep water. To provide storage, manufacturing and administration space, 56 buildings were erected. In addition, 13,638,450 square feet of open-storage space was graded and paved or provided with racks.

By June, the Advance Base Depot was in operation, and by the end of the year, a total of 286,000 tons of materiel had been shipped to overseas navy bases. The navy shipped even more vehicles, fuel storage equipment and other cargo per year to overseas bases during the height of the war.

Once war was declared on December 8, 1941, the Naval Air Station at Quonset Point served on the front lines of the war against German U-boats, a number of which prowled shipping lanes off Long Island, Cape Cod and northward. Numerous land-based and carrier-based antisubmarine squadrons trained and shipped out from Quonset. Sean Paul Mulligan, author of two books on the Quonset Point Naval Air Station, wrote that half of all German U-boats sunk by U.S. Navy planes in the North Atlantic were neutralized by Quonset-trained shore- and carrier-based squadrons. Many convoys were also protected from harm by Quonset-trained air crews.

In addition to training, pilots also flew on missions to seek and destroy U-boats from Quonset itself. For these missions, pilots often flew the most effective antisubmarine aircraft, Consolidated PB4Y-1s, the navy's designation for B-24 Liberators. These huge, four-engine, long-range bombers had been built for the U.S. Army but were handed over to the navy and modified for use in antisubmarine patrols. If an enemy submarine was spotted, the aircraft had a powerful searchlight mounted under the right wing that could shine on the U-boat. The pilot could then fly the plane over its target and release bombs for submarines still on the surface or depth charges if the U-boat had submerged.

Pilots frequently flew Lockheed PV-1 Venturas—twin-engine bombers that also carried rockets capable of penetrating a U-boat's hull—on antisubmarine flights from Quonset. There were also elegant Martin PBM Mariner flying boats and Consolidated PBY-5A Catalina flying boats, which could take off or

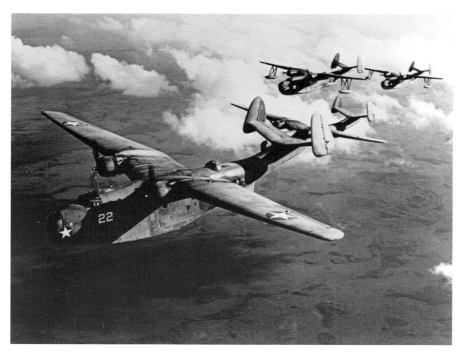

Two PBM-1 Mariners lead two PBM-3 Mariners, October 7, 1943. These "flying boats," frequently seen over Narragansett Bay, were secured in seaplane hangars at Quonset Point. *Naval History and Heritage Command.*

land on water in Narragansett Bay and use the seaplane hangar at Quonset. Most of these "sub-killers" were painted dull gull gray, the camouflage color for antisubmarine aircraft fighting in the Battle of the Atlantic. Aircraft from Quonset typically patrolled as far south as Montauk Point on Long Island and as far north as Martha's Vineyard and Nantucket.

On April 12, 1943, a lightly armed Kingfisher from Quonset Point unsuccessfully attacked German U-boat *U-161* about seventy-five miles south of Nantucket Shoals. One PBM Mariner, flying from Quonset on August 7, 1943, was one of several U.S. aircraft engaged in a six-hour shootout with German U-boat *U-566* off the coast of New Jersey, during which two Venturas flying from Floyd Bennett Field in New York were shot down. The Quonset-based Mariner came close to sinking the submarine with its bombs, but the enemy vessel ultimately escaped. These were some of the only antisubmarine combat missions pilots flying from Quonset Point had in the war. They could claim no kills of German submarines. They also provided air cover for convoys of merchant ships to pass safely in their patrol area.

The most important development in the U.S. Navy during World War II was the rise of the aircraft carrier. Fighter aircraft and bombers flying off carriers were the keys to U.S. naval victory in the Pacific and were important in winning the Battle of the Atlantic against German submarines. During the war, aircraft carriers visited Quonset to pick up aircraft and their pilots.

In 1944, seven escort (or baby) carriers were serviced at Quonset, each typically carrying just eight fighters and twelve torpedo/dive bombers. After departing, they sailed out in search of German U-boats, often with success. Ideally, on antisubmarine patrols from escort carriers, F4F Wildcats would sweep in on a German U-boat, firing their machine guns to suppress the enemy's antiaircraft defenses. Then, TBM Avengers would roll in to finish off the submarine with torpedoes or bombs or with depth charges if the submarine submerged. Of the eleven escort carriers that operated in the Atlantic, German submarines sank only one, USS *Block Island*, named after an island off Rhode Island, on May 29, 1944. Fortunately, only six of the crew were lost in the sinking off the Canary Islands. Before it was sunk, this carrier was credited with destroying two U-boats and shared in the credit for sinking two others. (In 1945, escort carriers moored down the bay at Newport rather than Quonset.)

It appears that only one large aircraft carrier visited Quonset during the war, USS *Ranger*, the only large carrier in the Atlantic Fleet. (After the war ended, other large carriers that had operated in the Pacific frequently visited Quonset.) *Ranger* typically had aboard about fifty-seven navy aircraft. In mid-

1942, it made some unusual voyages in support of the worldwide Allied war effort. After the first TBF Avengers successfully landed on its deck from Quonset Point on April 14, while moored at Quonset, *Ranger* loaded seventy-six army P-40 Warhawk fighter planes and men of the army's Thirty-Third Pursuit Squadron. The carrier put to sea on April 22, 1942, and escaping pursuing German U-boats, it launched the P-40s on May 10, where they safely landed at a U.S. air base at Accra, on the Gold Coast of Africa. *Ranger* then returned to Quonset Point on May 28 but not before having avoided another German submarine following it, sunk by an escorting destroyer the day before. Next, on June 2, the carrier made an antisubmarine patrol to Argentia, Newfoundland, Canada, returning to Quonset Point on June 22. Loading seventy-two P-40s and the accompanying Fifty-Seventh Fighter Group, *Ranger* steamed out of Narragansett Bay on July 1 and launched the P-40s off the coast of Africa for Accra on July 19, where they all landed safely. Both groups of P-40s were in route to support the Flying Tigers in China. On each of these three missions, *Ranger* was escorted by the flagship heavy cruiser USS *Augusta* and several destroyers, all operating out of Newport.

In November 1942, *Ranger* saw heavy fighting during the invasion of North Africa, and in October 1943, its Dauntless and Avenger dive bombers sank twenty-three thousand tons of German shipping in a raid in the North Sea. On January 11, 1944, the carrier docked at Quonset, where it was used for training purposes for three months. A sailor on board the carrier, Ernest Crochet, kept a journal of his service, and noted a total of 310 plane crashes during air operations off and on the carrier (several at Quonset), involving thirty-nine fatalities. He also counted forty-four contacts with German submarines by the carrier and its escorts.

A large portion of the pilots flying off aircraft carriers in the Pacific war against Japan were trained at Quonset. Those flying on dive bombers often trained on heavily armed Curtiss SB2C Helldivers. They also flew the navy's most ubiquitous plane, the Grumman F6F Hellcat fighter/dive bomber. Pilots flying torpedo bombers trained at Quonset from 1943 to the end of the war, mostly flying the successful Grumman TBF/TBM Avengers. Quonset also had on hand air-sea rescue and observation seaplanes called Vought OS2U Kingfishers.

According to historian Sean Paul Mulligan, commander, Fleet Air Quonset (COMFAIR Quonset) established at Quonset twenty-seven fast carrier bombing squadrons, forty-two fast carrier fighting squadrons, eleven escort carrier fighting squadrons, twenty fast carrier fighter bomber squadrons, more than twenty fast carrier night fighting squadrons and sixty-

Four Grumman TBF Avengers fly in formation over the control tower at NAS Quonset Point during the war. The navy's principal torpedo and dive bomber, TBF/TBM Avengers were the most common type of plane flown from Quonset Point. *U.S. Navy booklet on U.S. Naval Air Station Quonset Point, circa 1944, in the author's collection.*

one torpedo bombing squadrons. Most saw heavy action in the Pacific or in Europe. Planes established in groups and squadrons at Quonset were adorned on their tails with a "K" standing for Quonset.

The number of naval aircraft stationed at Quonset Point was surprisingly low in 1942 but had jumped markedly by mid-1943 and increased to spectacular heights by late 1943. Official U.S. Navy reports of locations of its aircraft showed only 4 at Quonset on February 22, 1942, increasing to 55 in April 1942 (when *Ranger* was in Narragansett Bay) but with only 52 there on December 8, 1942. By May 31, 1943, there were 132 navy aircraft located at the station, and from that date the numbers increased dramatically: 335 navy aircraft were reported to be at Quonset on January 5, 1944; 268 on May 16, 1944; and 350 on December 12, 1944. Most of the increase was attributable to the arrival of more torpedo/dive bombers and fighters, increasing from 24 at the end of 1942 to 294 at the end of 1944. As the war wound down, there were still 227 aircraft at Quonset on April

15, 1945. (See Appendix A for the number and types of aircraft at the air station on these dates.) These numbers correspond with national production of military aircraft, which was slow to ramp up in 1942 but got rolling by mid-1943.

These navy reports did not list training, army or other non-navy airplanes. There are indications that even more planes were located at the air station. In October 1943, the Quonset Point commander complained that the station was overcrowded with more than four hundred aircraft. An unidentified officer wrote at about the same time, "The traffic at Quonset is getting worse and worse. We have an *average* of 130 takeoffs and landings per hour over a ten-hour period from 0800 to 1800 one day. 660 aircraft on the station on April 1. What a place!"

Prior to World War II, few Americans had flown in airplanes, much less flown them. Inevitably, with all of these planes being flown, many by young and relatively inexperienced pilots in rapidly built airplanes that did not yet have many safety features, coupled with the sometimes poor New England weather, accidents occurred. "More Hellcats were lost in Rhode Island through training mishaps than were shot down in air-to-air combat with the Japanese," commented Mulligan. With luck, three or four days would go by at Quonset without an aircraft accident, he added.

Sometimes the accidents were fatal. For example, on Saturday afternoon, April 22, 1944, two Hellcats assigned to the same squadron collided in midair over the Quonset Manor neighborhood of North Kingstown. Both pilots were killed. One plane sheared the tail off the other while both planes were several hundred feet in the air. One of the Hellcats, piloted by twenty-two-year-old Ensign Joseph Clyde Rust, of Alliance, Nebraska, crashed on King Phillip Drive and exploded. The other Hellcat, piloted by twenty-one-year-old Ensign Oswald Eugene Asplund Jr. of Glenview, Illinois, crashed in Sawmill Pond.

Crashing into Rhode Island's freshwater ponds and swamps was not uncommon—two sank in Warden's Pond in Wakefield alone. A Curtiss SB2C-4 Helldiver was removed from it around 1963. Civilians on the ground were also not always immune from harm. According to journalist Gerald Carbone, one Quonset pilot "smashed into a house in Coventry and killed a man's family while he was at work."

Jim Ignasher, in his book *Rhode Island Disasters*, describes fatal accidents, crashes and disappearances of four planes flying from or to the Naval Air Station at Quonset Point. In one accident on the morning of December 5, 1943, after a practice flight above Block Island Sound, a PV-1 Ventura,

Small aircraft carriers called escort carriers, similar to the USS *Block Island* pictured here in 1943, picked up planes and pilots at Quonset Point before heading out in search of German submarines. *Naval History and Heritage Command.*

attempting to land at Quonset, accidentally crashed into a hangar. The entire six-man crew perished. On March 30, 1943, a Grumman Hellcat on a routine flight from the aircraft carrier USS *Ranger* off the coast of Massachusetts heading to Quonset disappeared in a storm that unexpectedly swept through southern New England; it has never been found. It could be that the aircraft flew into one of Rhode Island's many freshwater lakes or reservoirs. On the night of January 31, 1944, in snowy weather with strong wind gusts, a PB4Y-1 left Quonset with a crew of ten men and was never heard from again. The missing sub-killer was finally located in 1992 at the bottom of Block Island Sound about thirteen miles off Block Island. On the morning of June 6, 1944, a PV-1 departed Quonset and, apparently primarily due to pilot error, crashed into the Dumplings, an outcropping of rocks off the southern tip of Jamestown facing Breton Point. All seven men on board perished.

There is one continuing reminder that more than twenty Royal Navy squadrons were also trained at Quonset to fly American-built planes. Tucked away in a corner of Island Cemetery in Newport are the graves of eight British and Commonwealth officers and enlisted men who died while in the United States in 1943 and one in 1944. Most of them were killed as a result of training accidents while flying in the local area. For example, on June 15, 1943, Morgan Douglas Hamilton lost control of his F4U Corsair during takeoff, left the runway and crashed into a bomb bunker. His plane then exploded, killing him and injuring twenty-four others. Lieutenant Charles Newton Lovely, a twenty-one-year-old Londoner, was on a routine flight on July 21, 1943, when his Corsair caught fire and he was forced to bail out over the Sakonnet River. His parachute failed to open, and he fell to his death. The Royal Navy graves are located on Evarts Street along the fence line in a small section of the Island Cemetery at the corner of Brandt Street and Van Zandt Avenue, Navy Section Plots 172–177, graves 12–20.

Commissioned on April 1, 1943, at Quonset Point, the U.S. Navy Aircraft Anti-Submarine Development Detachment brought together naval pilots, technicians and scientists to develop antisubmarine warfare techniques. On the cutting edge of research in airborne radar and electronics systems, it helped develop new high-resolution airborne radars to fight enemy submarines. A team of twenty-five Quonset researchers also developed magnetic anomaly detection (MAD) gear, which could detect minute variations in the earth's magnetic field, such as an underwater submarine or a submarine that had surfaced at night. On October 21, 1941, a PBY from Quonset detected a submerged American submarine using MAD gear, the first successful test of the newly developed equipment. As detecting an enemy submarine could be realized only by operators after a plane using MAD equipment had flown over it, "retro rockets" were designed to fly backward to where the submarine was detected. Beginning in early 1944, aircraft using this technology was effectively used against German submarines attempting to move through the Straits of Gibraltar, and a retro rocket fired by a Catalina helped to sink *U-761*. The MAD equipment, with antisubmarine retro rockets, was often flown on PBY-5A Catalina seaplanes from Quonset. The top-secret Spraycliff Observatory, located near Beavertail Point in Jamestown, was where much of the radar and magnetic equipment was developed by some of the nation's top physicists.

In 1942, a naval aircraft rework facility for the repair and overhaul of aircraft engines and airframes opened at Quonset. Thousands of local civilian men and women were hired for the work. One of them, Marie Duggins, a WAVE from Connecticut, was embarrassed by the "hollering and cat-call whistles from the sailors" when she first arrived with other WAVES at

Quonset Point and marched with them to the mess hall. But she settled in and became adept at cleaning the rust from engine parts by soaking them in large vats of chemicals. Workers in the A&R Shop operated eighteen hours a day, seven days a week. In March 1945, they completed major overhauls of 163 engines, 10 more than the previous month. In October 1942, the A&R Shop began to recruit women to fill new positions. By July 1943, 40 percent of its civilian employees were female, and nearly two hundred women had a rating of mechanic or mechanic's helper.

Quonset Point also had a Naval Training School for newly minted navy officers. Called indoctrination training, the object was to give newly commissioned officers a basic knowledge of naval customs, nomenclature, military law, hygiene and drill. The short program's most famous graduate was twenty-nine-year-old Richard Nixon, who, following his appointment as lieutenant junior grade in the U.S. Naval Reserve, began indoctrination training in August 1942. When Nixon became president, he appointed as his secretary of state William Rogers. Nixon once joked about Rogers, "We met thirty-two years ago at Quonset Point when we were both one of the lowest

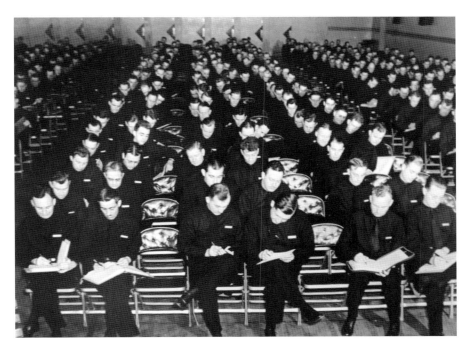

Navy reserve officers take a test during an indoctrination course at Quonset Point in 1944. *From a Navy Reserve 1944 publication held by the Naval War College Archives..*

forms of life, I mean lieutenants, junior grade, in the United States Navy Reserve." One classmate of the two called their training "very demanding physically and mentally." More than seven thousand men took the course before the program ended in February 1944.

Some of the top graduates, a total of 1,448 of them, received further training at the U.S. Naval Air Combat Information School at Quonset. Many went on to serve on carriers in the Pacific. One graduate was already famous—Hollywood actor Henry Fonda graduated fourth out of forty-one officer candidates in late 1944.

Another trainee attracting attention was William Patrick Hitler, whose father was Adolf Hitler's older half-brother. After interviewing him, the FBI decided to permit the nephew of the hated dictator to serve in the U.S. Navy. Trained at Davisville in 1944, William honorably served three years as a pharmacist's mate, receiving the Purple Heart for a wound he suffered.

To increase training opportunities for pilots, three auxiliary airfields were established to support Quonset Point, one at Martha's Vineyard, one at Westerly and the largest at Charlestown. In addition to those Naval Auxiliary Air Facilities (as they were officially called, or NAAFs), by mid-1944 the commander at Quonset Point also commanded NAAFs at Hyannis on Cape Cod (Otis Field), Sandwich, Nantucket Island, New Bedford and Plymouth in Massachusetts, Groton in Connecticut and Beavertail Point in Rhode Island. (The latter did not contain an airfield.)

The airfields at Charlestown and Westerly initially supported the training of carrier pilots. Some 600 acres at Charlestown were acquired by the navy in 1940, work was authorized in October 1942, and the field was completed in June 1943. Three asphalt runways were built at Charlestown, one 5,800 feet long, a second 5,470 feet long and a third 4,800 feet long, in addition to a catapult and arresting gear system to simulate carrier takeoffs and landings. The navy also took over the small civilian Westerly Airport, paved the dirt runway and expanded it to 419 acres.

The bases began operation in June 1943. On January 5, 1944, Charlestown had only 48 naval aircraft and Westerly 14 aircraft. Those numbers quickly increased to impressive numbers: 96 and 13, respectively, by May 16, 1944; 158 and 41 on December 12, 1944; and 133 and 29 on April 15, 1945. The vast majority of the planes were F6F Hellcat fighters. (See Appendix A.) In early 1944, the barracks at Charlestown bulged with 269 officers and 1,751 men.

Pilots, such as future U.S. president George H.W. Bush, trained for aircraft carrier landings and takeoffs at Charlestown. On his eighteenth birthday, June 12, 1942, Bush enlisted in the navy, becoming its youngest pilot. Assigned as

Aerial view of the three runways at the Naval Auxiliary Air Facilities at Charlestown, circa 1944. *Naval War College Archives.*

a bomber and aerial photography pilot on a TBF-1 Avenger torpedo and dive bomber on the newly commissioned aircraft carrier USS *San Jacinto*, he wound up at Charlestown for his final training. Navy records indicate that his squadron, VT-51, arrived at Charlestown between November 30 and December 7, 1943, and departed between January 18 and January 25, 1944. Bush wrote from Charlestown on December 12, 1943, to his fiancée, Barbara, "The wind of late has been blowing like mad and our flying has been cut to a minimum. My plane, #2 now, is up at Quonset, having a camera installed." In late January, Ensign Bush and the rest of his squadron flew their planes to Norfolk, Virginia, and then onto the *San Jacinto* for the first time, landing on the carrier while it was at sea. Bush wrote to his parents, "We, the TBFs, landed first. The ship looked really swell steaming along in her battle camouflage. We made a few practice passes down wind and then she swung around into the wind and we came aboard. She was moving at a good clip and the air was nice and smooth, facilitating the landings. We each made 3 landings and then cut our motors on the deck."

On September 2, 1944, Bush flew his Avenger off the *San Jacinto* to bomb a Japanese radio installation at the Pacific island of Chichi Jima. His plane was struck by Japanese antiaircraft fire, but Bush forged ahead, dropping his bombs on the target. Shortly afterward, over the Pacific Ocean and with his cockpit filling with smoke, he ordered his crew to abandon the plane. He jumped out and was rescued by a submarine. To Bush's great sadness, the bodies of his talented radio man, Jack Delaney of Providence, and two others, were never recovered.

Charlestown and Westerly also specialized in night fighter training, which was transferred from Quonset Point in late 1943. Hellcats were first equipped with special radar for night fighting in April 1944. Early in the war, Japanese pilots had the ability to attack U.S. Navy ships at night, while American pilots lacked these skills. In October 1944, Japanese pilots began kamikaze suicide attacks on ships and quickly showed a preference for attacking at night. In response, the training of night fighter squadrons operating from carriers became the highest priority. In November 1944, the U.S. Navy formed the Night Attack and Combat Training Unit-Atlantic at Charlestown, the East Coast's primary one. Most pilots at the time flew "by the seat of their pants," based on what they could see. But that did not help in foggy conditions or at night. Pilots at Charlestown specialized in flying in the dark using cockpit instruments only, and radar improved at the Spraycliff Observatory in Jamestown to detect enemy fighters. They trained at night and slept during the day. Under the guidance of Commander William E.G. Taylor, the night fighter pilots developed into an elite corps of flyers.

There were more fatal accidents at Charlestown, especially with the risky night fighter training. For example, in 1944, twenty-two-year-old Ensign James Gannon of Jersey City, New Jersey, died after his Grumman F6F-3N Hellcat night fighter crashed in the Kenyon section of Charlestown, charring ten acres of woods. It was sometimes difficult to recover all the remains of a pilot who had crashed. According to one pilot who trained at Charlestown during the war, it was standard procedure to place what remained of a dead pilot into a coffin with a few sacks of concrete spread evenly to simulate the weight of a whole man. A memorial was erected at the former Charlestown airfield (after the war called a station and later a landing field) commemorating sixty-two airmen who lost their lives during its existence from 1943 to 1965. Three died in 1943, twenty-two in 1944 and twenty-four in 1945.

4

Seabees, Pontoons and Quonset Huts at Davisville

By Christian McBurney

In North Kingstown, next door to the Naval Air Station at Quonset Point, was Camp Endicott at Davisville, the country's principal base for naval construction battalions that became known as the Seabees. Davisville and Quonset Point also gave rise to two spectacular developments during the war: the pontoon and the Quonset hut.

Until 1942, the U.S. Navy had relied on civilian contractors to build its combat bases and airfields. But after Pearl Harbor, the use of civilian labor in war zones became impractical. Under international law, civilians who fought in battle could be executed as guerrillas. To defeat Japan, the navy needed a military construction force that could build on isolated islands and fight at the same time. On December 28, 1941, Rear Admiral Ben Moreell, chief of the Bureau of Yards and Docks, requested specific authority to activate and organize such an outfit, called the naval construction battalions. On January 5, 1942, he was granted that authority, and many of the original battalions formed at a new U.S. Navy base in Davisville, Rhode Island.

Many of the first recruits to this new outfit were the men who had helped to build Boulder Dam, the national highways and New York City skyscrapers; had worked in mines and quarries or dug subway tunnels; and had worked in shipyards. Some sixty-one trades were represented. Recruits were permitted to be up to fifty years old so that experienced workers could be obtained. The Seabees built military bases for U.S. forces around the world and constructed thousands of miles of roads, including in Alaska and Canada.

Review of the Seventy-First, Seventy-Seventh and Eighty-First Naval Construction Battalions at Camp Endicott, May 8, 1943. *Naval War College Museum Collections.*

The Seabee base at Davisville was opened in stages, with training for the first 296 men beginning in February 1942. Some two hundred buildings, most of them wood, were constructed on the 250-acre site, located north of the Naval Air Station at Quonset Point and southwest of the Advance Base Depot. It was officially dedicated on June 27, 1942—at a ceremony attended by Secretary of the Navy Frank Knox—and named Camp Endicott on August 11, 1942. Officially, Camp Endicott was called the Naval Construction Training Center. The capacity of the base—ten battalions in training, totaling approximately 350 officers and 15,000 men—was reached early in November 1942. During World War II, 325,000 enlisted men and 7,960 officers served with the Seabees, with more than 100,000 of them trained at Davisville. All nationwide Seabee training, including officer training, was carried out on at Camp Endicott starting in June 1944.

The six-week technical training at Camp Endicott included twenty-seven courses teaching skills ranging from diving to bulldozer operation. Military training included judo, close-order drill and the use of various weapons. As battalions completed their training, many were sent for more training next door at the Advance Base Depot, where mockups of Liberty ships were built so that Seabees could train loading them.

"I was here at Quonset when the first Seabees came, and I was a civilian worker," said Robert Mellor, then of Wakefield. He quickly joined up with the Seabees, and after a training stint at Quonset Point, was island hopping with the marines from the first big land battle of the Pacific—Guadalcanal— to one of the last—the liberation of the Philippines. He was a surveyor, helping with the construction of airstrips, temporary barracks and hospitals.

The Seabees name and logo originated at Quonset Point. Frank J. Iafrate, a North Providence native, then just nineteen years old, was working as a civilian file clerk at the Naval Air Station at Quonset and, after becoming known for drawing caricatures, in early January 1942 was asked to produce a logo for the new outfit. The Seabees name derived from pronouncing the letters *CB*, short for Construction Battalion. Iafrate came up with the idea of a zooming, hardworking bee. "The rest came easily," recalled Iafrate later. "I gave the bee a white sailor's cap, various tools to show his construction talents and finally a tommy gun to show his fighting ability." Iafrate did the work in three hours on a Sunday afternoon. After viewing it, Rear Admiral Moreell adopted it and called off a nationwide campaign he had planned for creating a logo. The name Seabee was also officially adopted. Iafrate joined the Seabees in August 1942 and trained at Camp Endicott. (In 1971 Iafrate also later drew plans for a brightly colored metal sculpture of a tommy gun—

The Seabees insignia designed by Frank Iafrate of North Providence in 1941, showing a bee carrying a tommy gun and tools. *Naval History and Heritage Command*.

and tool-toting Seabee mascot bee, which stood guard at the base entrance for more than twenty-five years.)

Camp Thomas, occupying 142 acres and eventually containing some five hundred Quonset huts, was established in Davisville, north of Camp Endicott, on October 23, 1943. It provided temporary housing for Seabees either arriving at Davisville from other boot camps for further training or overseas deployment, or returning to Davisville after tours of duty. It also contained a one-hundred- by forty-two-foot Quonset hut that served as a chapel for members of the Catholic, Protestant and Jewish faiths.

Through the war years, navy personnel at the twenty-three-acre Advance Base Proving Ground at Allen Harbor in Davisville tested and developed hundreds of pieces of equipment for navy use, including distillation units, filtration units, laundry equipment, stoves, propulsion units, trucks and generators and many pontoon assemblies. Work on pontoon bridges began at Quonset even before the U.S. declared war and was relocated to Allen Harbor in the spring of 1943. By the next year, workers there had developed—in addition to pontoon bridges—floating dry docks, barges, causeways and piers

A pier is in the early stages of construction, and dredging operations are shown at the Advance Base Proving Ground at Allen Harbor, June 1943. The upper left shows pontoon storage. *U.S. Navy/Seabee Museum.*

that were eventually used in the U.S. war effort in North Africa, Europe and the Pacific. The floating pontoon causeways were crucial to the invasions of Sicily and Anzio in Italy, North Africa and Normandy, France. In December 1943, the largest floating airfield structure in the world, more than 1,800 feet long, was assembled and tested at the Advance Base Proving Ground.

With the Seabees and their new pontoon causeways, which Seabees could construct in under ten minutes and use to transport tanks and trucks from ship to shore, the Allies were able to carry off a surprise attack on weakly defended Sicilian beaches. The enemy was quickly outflanked and overpowered as large numbers of men and huge amounts of equipment poured ashore over pontoon causeways. On March 22, 1945, Seabees built pontoon ferries that were used to transport the tanks of General George Patton across the Rhine River at Oppenheim in a frontal assault that swept away the surprised German defenders.

Military planners realized that with the tremendous increase in military personnel, supplies and equipment, they needed a way to house people and store materiel at far-flung military bases. The buildings needed to be inexpensive, lightweight and portable so they could be shipped anywhere and put up quickly using hand tools. The British had developed a light, prefabricated structure called a Nissen hut during World War I, but its design was inadequate for needs in the 1940s.

In March 1941, the Fuller Company, busy constructing the Naval Air Station at Quonset Point, was asked to design and produce a hut to U.S. military specification and to do it within two months. Fuller engineer Peter Dejongh and the company's only staff architect, Otto Brandenberger, adapted the British Nissen hut design using corrugated steel and semicircular arched steel ribs and made other major improvements. The Anderson Sheet

Quonset huts lined up at the Motor Torpedo Boat Squadrons Training Center in Melville, summer of 1942. *Naval History and Heritage Command*.

Metal Company of Providence solved the technical problem of bending the corrugated sheets into usable shapes that were then attached with nuts and bolts. The two ends were covered with plywood that had doors and windows.

Fuller quickly set up a production facility on eighty-five acres at West Davisville. A navy engineer, Commander R.V. Miler, came up with the idea of naming the huts after the location where they were designed—since the area was known as Quonset Point, the new design was called a Quonset hut.

Remarkably, the first hut was produced within sixty days of the contract award. In June 1941, the navy sent its first shipment of Quonset huts overseas.

There was concern that since the curved line of the sidewalls began at the floor, there would be a loss of effective width of the hut. A second version of the Quonset hut included a four-foot-high vertical sidewall, or knee wall. In addition, the T-rib huts were difficult to crate and heavy to ship. Engineers developed lightweight steel that replaced the heavier T-rib units. Anyone who could hammer a nail could set it up. A crew of only six experienced men could build a hut in a single day.

As finally developed, the Quonset hut required less shipping space than did tents with wood floors and frames. The flexible open interior space of a Quonset hut allowed it to be used for dozens of applications, including

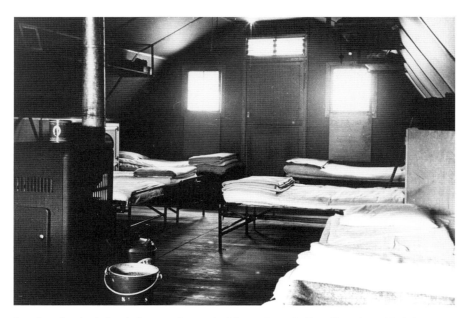

Interior of a single-bunk Quonset hut at the Motor Torpedo Boat Squadrons Training Center in Melville, circa 1944. *Naval History and Heritage Command.*

barracks, mess halls, hospitals, storage facilities, administrative offices, medical and dental offices, isolation wards, classrooms, dormitories, bakeries, chapels, theaters and latrines.

Quonset huts bound for Europe and other northern climates had fixed wood bulkheads, insulation and windows. The tropical hut had screen bulkheads, screen windows, removable side segments and a lifting top section that provided additional ventilation. Complaints were made that they were either too hot or too cold.

Quonset huts typically ranged from twenty by forty feet to forty by one hundred feet. The largest wartime Quonset was built on Guam, a fifty-four-thousand-square-foot warehouse.

More than 32,000 Quonset huts were manufactured at Fuller's West Davisville factory and sent overseas during World War II. Production of the huts was eventually moved to private steel firms in the Midwest, Mississippi and California, where some 120,000 more were manufactured.

Quonset huts were commonly used in Rhode Island. For example, 154 huts were built at the Motor Torpedo Boat Squadrons Training Center in Melville, and 286 were constructed at or near Coddington Point to accommodate the influx of new trainees at the Naval Training Station in Newport.

After the war, the Quonset hut became the inspiration for modern prefabricated metal construction. While Quonset huts never became popular with the civilian population, a Pittsburgh company continues to manufacture them today.

The PT Boat Training Center at Melville

By Brian L. Wallin

Five miles north of the Newport Naval Base, at the small village of Melville in Portsmouth, few traces remain of what was the country's primary World War II training center for PT (patrol torpedo) boat crews. The only visible evidence of the Motor Torpedo Boat Squadrons Training Center is a bronze monument flanked by a 40-millimeter gun and a torpedo. PT Boats Incorporated, a national organization with the mission of preserving PT boat history, placed the marker in 1976 to honor PT boaters killed in action during the war. The wording on the plaque eloquently sums up the impact of the center:

> *A rigid schedule trained landlubbers for the strenuous, hazardous duty on board "fifty tons of fighting fury" for combat in every theater of World War II. They were taught engineering, gunnery, navigation, seamanship, communications, supply and survival. Glued and screwed together, 80 feet of wood had to operate against the enemy from the tropics to the Arctic. By the end of World War II, more than 14,000 officers and men had been trained here.*
>
> *The record shows the training was most effective. From this group has come a president of the United States of America, senators and congressmen, a United States Supreme Court Justice, U.S. ambassadors, governors, judges, mayors, presidents of large corporations, movie stars, and thousands of 100 percent patriotic Americans, PT Boaters all.*

A PT boat from Melville with the Mount Hope Bridge in the background, March 1944. *PT Boats Incorporated.*

The president, of course, was John F. Kennedy, who often proudly recounted his service as a PT boat skipper in the Pacific. And it brought him the attention of the national public for the first time. The August 2, 1943 ramming of his *PT-109* by a Japanese destroyer and the dramatic rescue of Kennedy and most of his crew have been immortalized in print and on film. Kennedy entered the PT school at Melville on October 1, 1942, after meeting the navy requirements for PT boat recruits of being intelligent and athletic and having experience with small boats. (Kennedy was an avid sailor.) Before leaving on his fateful cruise aboard *PT-109*, Kennedy picked for his crew replacements recently arrived from Melville.

Kennedy contributed a foreword to retired navy captain Robert Bulkley Jr.'s 1962 definitive PT history, *At Close Quarters, PT Boats in the United States Navy*, writing, "Small as they were, the PT boats played a key role." He continued:

> *Like most naval ships, they could carry out numerous tasks with dispatch and versatility. In narrow waters or in fighting close to land they could deliver a powerful punch with torpedo or gun. On occasion, they could lay mines or drop depth charges. They could speed through reefs and shark-infested waters to rescue downed pilots or secretly close to shore to make contacts with coast watchers and guerilla forces. PT boats were an embodiment of John Paul Jones' words "I wish to have no connection with any ship that does not sail fast for I intend to go in harm's way."*

By the end of the war, more than 650 PT boats had been commissioned, and forty-four squadrons (with an average of 12 boats per squadron) had served from the Pacific to the Mediterranean, from D-day to Guadalcanal and even in the Arctic. Most of their crews (but not all) passed through Melville's training center and repair school. During their sixty days (later expanded to ninety days) of training, they were taught every aspect of the handling and care of the small warships.

During the war years, the thunderous roar of these tough little heavily armed vessels were familiar sounds to Rhode Islanders, who often saw them speeding in formation up and down Narragansett Bay at around forty miles per hour. Too small to be christened as named ships, they were carried on the navy's rolls by number. But their crews bestowed colorful nicknames, such as "Aces & Eights," "Flying Shamrock," "Rapid Robert" and "Ole Spooky."

At first armed with a pair of dual .50-caliber machine guns and four torpedo tubes, the boats gradually added a variety of armaments. These included 20-, 37- and 40-millimeter guns, depth charges and, later in the war, mortars and primitive rockets. The torpedo tubes at first fired leftover World War I Mark VIII submarine torpedoes, but they were later supplied with the effective Mark XIII aircraft torpedoes, all from the Naval Torpedo Station at Newport. Eventually, the tubes were replaced by roll-off launching devices invented by PT boaters and approved for use after testing at Melville.

Starting with a British-designed seventy-foot PT boat, a few American companies began manufacturing and testing PT boats in the 1930s. In the summer of 1941, an intense competition among manufacturers to further refine the abilities of the boats was held off the coasts of Connecticut and Block Island. Because of the PTs' wooden construction, the trials were popularly known as the "plywood derby" (the boats were actually solidly built of laminated mahogany). The navy zeroed in on the larger seventy-seven-foot and eighty-foot models, which were more seaworthy and better able to accommodate the navy's stock of older Mark VIII torpedoes than smaller models.

PT crews of two officers and twelve enlisted men were initially all volunteers (later some replacements were drawn directly from the fleet). Most of the officers were reservists, college graduates who had sped through Naval Reserve Midshipmen Schools at college campuses around the country. Many were Ivy Leaguers, who, like Kennedy, had prior sailing experience.

After the Japanese struck Pearl Harbor on December 7, 1941, navy brass decided that they needed hundreds of PTs to operate in the numerous small and isolated islands of the Pacific. It was also recognized that formal training

Aerial view of the motor torpedo boat squadrons training center in 1945, showing numerous Quonset huts and PT boats docked in the cove. *Naval War College Museum Collections.*

was needed for the PT crews to handle and maintain these unique craft.

On January 13, 1942, Motor Torpedo Boat Squadron Four was created and sent to the Newport Naval Base. It would remain the largest PT squadron, reaching a peak of twenty-eight boats in Melville and representing all types of PT boat models in commission. This squadron supported the training program through the end of the war and also patrolled the waters off the coasts of Rhode Island and southeastern Massachusetts. As the war progressed, it was staffed by returning PT veterans, as well as recent training school graduates, who were often reluctant to remain since they were anxious to get to war zones.

On February 17, 1942, Secretary of the Navy Frank Knox directed the establishment of a permanent PT training program in Narragansett Bay reporting to Admiral Edward C. Kalbfus, commandant of Naval Operating Base Newport. As Newport was crowded with other naval facilities, Melville was selected as the site for PT boat training.

The exact reason that Aquidneck Island was chosen has been lost to history, but several factors likely came into play. First, Newport was already one of the navy's most important training centers, and it had at its disposal well-protected Narragansett Bay. It was also a relatively short cruise from a major PT boat factory in New Jersey, as well as to the New York Navy Yard, where the PTs were fitted out. At Melville, new systems could be tested and the crew familiarized with their new craft in "shakedown" cruises. (Boats built in far-off shipyards underwent trials close to their construction sites, but crews were still trained in Rhode Island.)

Locating PT training on Aquidneck Island was convenient because the torpedoes PTs used for practice were built at the Torpedo Station on Newport's Goat Island. In addition, PTs were powered by three 1,500-horsepower Packard engines requiring 100-octane fuel, which was in ready supply at the Naval Fuel Depot at Melville.

Each training class consisted of twenty officers and eighty enlisted men. Officers, many of whom had never been to sea, were trained in navigation, gunnery and small boat handling. Enlisted personnel were trained in weaponry, engine operation and maintenance, radio and radar and small boat handling.

The navy tapped Lieutenant William C. Specht, a former PT boat squadron commander, to serve as the first commanding officer of the new Motor Torpedo Boat Squadrons Training Center at Melville. Arriving in Newport in March 1942, newly promoted to the rank of lieutenant commander, Specht also assumed command of Squadron Four. He was charged with developing a new training curriculum and overseeing the construction of an entirely new base at Melville.

Construction got underway immediately. While a Massachusetts company began the initial work, over the next couple of years, Rhode Island firms Gilbane Building Company, Coleman Construction and H.V. Collins, all of Providence, were brought in.

The original plan for the center called for 59 buildings of various sizes, but that number quickly was deemed insufficient. The base became largely a Quonset hut facility but included a number of wood and permanent brick or concrete structures. The prefabricated Quonset huts, also a product of Rhode Island (see chapter 4), served as living quarters, machine shops, classrooms, mess halls and warehouses. Eventually, some 150 Quonset huts were built at Melville.

The most challenging project was the boat basin, created from a lagoon that was underwater only at high tide. Obviously, that would not do. In April 1942, the lagoon was dammed up, existing water rerouted and a massive amount of soil dug out by heavy equipment. Eventually, some 300,000 cubic yards of dirt was moved. Enough dredging had been done by the end of July 1942 for the first PT boats to be motored into the basin the next month. Finger piers were later added, and the lagoon was further improved over the next few months.

The base was essentially complete by the fall of 1942. Specht was joined by a number of other PT officers and enlisted men who had gained experience at Pearl Harbor and in the Philippines. The Melville base was quickly and affectionately dubbed "Specht Tech."

Specht frequently greeted each new class of freshly minted ensigns, junior grade lieutenants and enlisted men of various ratings with these words: "There are vast numbers of young men throughout the country who would give a great deal to have the opportunity which is now yours—that of qualifying to operate and fight the finest motor torpedo boats the world has ever produced." Specht and his successors demanded high standards of the prospective PT boaters, as they would be called on to operate with considerable independence and frequently in both primitive and dangerous conditions.

The base was laid out along the Melville shoreline in a north–south direction, extending east to State Highway 114, at the time a main road from

Lieutenant Commander William Specht stands in front of the first class of officers graduating from the Motor Torpedo Boat Squadrons Training Center, April 1942. *National Archives*.

Providence to Newport. The base was also visible from Mount Hope Bridge, and PT boats soon became familiar sights from the bridge and shorelines as they raced up and down Narragansett Bay.

Melville included the features of any large military installation, including living quarters, shops, classrooms and large warehouses built along the waterfront. Recreational facilities included a ship's store (the navy's version of a PX), gymnasium and a fifty-meter swimming pool. The base had its own post office, fire station, chapel and a mess hall capable of serving 4,000 men in a ninety-minute period. To support the intensive training of thousands of men, the base staffing grew to 57 officers and some 280 enlisted men.

Recognizing the need to train crews in boat repair, often in remote locations, a Motor Torpedo Boat Repair Training Unit (MTBRTU) reporting to the training center commander was established on February 12, 1944, by order of Secretary of the Navy Frank Knox. The unit was set up on a hilltop overlooking the base in existing buildings formerly used by civilian contractors. As many as 30 officers and 950 enlisted men could be accommodated for a six-week course. New classes began monthly, with war-worn PT boats brought to Melville to serve as training platforms for students.

On board the PTs, three huge twelve-cylinder, 1,500-horsepower Packard engines were housed in the cramped engine compartment. Civilian engineers from Packard worked with the navy to create a training program in the operation, maintenance and replacement of the engines in the field. Many of the motor machinist mates who served as trainers had already been to the navy's diesel schools or the Packard motor school in Detroit. Building Number 7 at Melville was devoted to hands-on training, with the adjacent Building Number 6 set up to teach engine overhaul. An engineering building was used for teaching troubleshooting and repair techniques in the field.

The Naval Fuel Depot and Naval Net Depot at Melville both abutted and supported the Motor Torpedo Boat Squadrons Training Center. The Fuel Depot dated back to 1901 when the navy set up a coaling station to serve ships based at Newport. By 1931, it had fully transitioned to a supply center for fuel oil. In 1940, the navy set up an antisubmarine net and mine facility at Melville adjacent to the Fuel Depot. The two units shared the same commanding officer but had different missions. The Net Depot became the navy's main submarine net training school and also maintained and repaired nets, including those used by the U.S. Army for Narragansett Bay defenses.

All work and no recreation is not productive. The Melville base provided a variety of recreation activities, including swimming, bowling, USO dances and even entertainment shows put on by national radio programs. Baseball

PT boat trainees learning to use a .50-caliber machine gun. *Naval War College Museum Collections.*

and basketball teams competed in Rhode Island military leagues. The base had both officers' and enlisted men's clubs. Liberty was granted after the first month's training. Most PT boaters headed for nearby Providence, Newport or Fall River on their brief liberty passes, which restricted the men to a forty-mile radius around Melville.

Throughout its existence, Melville had only three commanding officers, all of whom had previous experience in PTs. Specht, who assumed command in March 1942, was succeeded in September 1943 by Commander David Walsh, who remained in the post until June 1945. Commander Thomas Warfield, the last commander, supervised the base's decommissioning on November 1, 1945.

Navy facilities near Melville supported the training program. Gunnery practice, for example, was provided at the navy's Anti-Aircraft Training Center on Price's Neck on Newport's Ocean Drive. PTs also conducted torpedo launch training in conjunction with the Torpedo Station's Gould Island facility.

PT boats motoring on Narragansett Bay were a common sight during World War II. *PT Boats Incorporated.*

Squadron Four patrolled the waters off Rhode Island's coastline, as did newly arrived PTs and their fledgling crews, thus providing them with additional experience. By 1943, all new squadrons were conducting their shakedown cruises at Melville, increasing the numbers of PTs seen around Narragansett Bay.

While all of these missions created a hive of activity, they also—on occasion—resulted in accidents. Fortunately, there are no recorded incidents involving serious casualties. In 1942, the skipper of *PT-122* was reprimanded for crossing into the torpedo launching range off Gould Island and narrowly avoiding being struck by a test torpedo that had just been fired. Apparently, the noise of the PT engines prevented those aboard from hearing the warning whistle sounded by the test station.

On April 9, 1942, *PT-59*, while heading down the East Passage of Narragansett Bay for routine torpedo practice, accidentally launched a live torpedo. The Mark VIII ran "straight and hot" some seven miles down the bay before it unluckily struck the stern of a cargo ship, the USS *Capella*, at the time anchored off Jamestown. The ship started to sink, but using his PT boat's powerful engines, the quick-thinking boat skipper nudged the damaged ship to shallow water and the shore. It was later repaired and returned to service. *PT-59* later successfully served in the Solomon Islands and at Guadalcanal. The incident remained classified until the 1970s.

In 1943, another Mark VIII launched by a PT boat traveled off course and struck a freighter anchored off the Naval Air Station at Quonset Point, but no material damage was done. In yet another incident, *PT-200*, on routine patrol off the Rhode Island coast, was rammed and sunk by an unknown vessel on February 22, 1944. The crew did not suffer any serious injuries.

When the war ended in 1945, reductions came quickly to Melville. Training was halted on August 20, 1945. By the fall, both the training and repair facilities had been decommissioned. Squadron Four was sent to Maryland before the end of the year. By 1947, the navy had sold off nearly all of the Quonset huts from the base. Other structures were gradually torn down—a few remained in use after the property was turned over to the State of Rhode Island and ultimately to private industry. The Net Depot was briefly reactivated during the Korean War, but it finally closed in 1959 when the navy phased out harbor net defense functions. The Fuel Depot ceased operations in 1998. Today, much of the area is home to privately owned pleasure and racing yacht buildings and marina storage companies.

The PTs left a proud legacy after World War II, much of it centered at Melville. Only a handful of PT boats from World War II remain today. Two of them have been lovingly restored and are on display at the National PT Boat Museum at Battleship Cove in Fall River. The museum also serves as a repository for many of the artifacts and records held by PT Boats Incorporated, a nonprofit organization established to keep the memory of these remarkable and highly effective small warships alive.

6

The Growth of Naval Activity and Its Effect on Aquidneck Island

By John W. Kennedy

The U.S. Navy, despite the obvious advantages of Narragansett Bay as a protected anchorage for large ships, did not establish a permanent presence in the bay until 1869. In that year, the Torpedo Station was constructed on Goat Island on land that came to the Navy Department from the War Department. In 1880, the electors of the city of Newport acquired Coasters Harbor Island for the purpose of turning it over to the navy to establish a Naval Training Station for new recruits. The Training Station was established in 1883 and the Naval War College in 1884. In 1896, state leaders enacted laws paving the way for the navy in 1900 to acquire land at Melville as a coaling station. This law was later amended in 1903, allowing the navy to purchase Government Landing, 4.7 acres in the heart of downtown Newport and, in 1909, to acquire property that became the Naval Hospital. During World War I and its aftermath, the Torpedo Station expanded to Rose Island and Gould Island, and 151 acres at Coddington Point were acquired to accommodate expansion for the naval training center.

In his fireside chat on June 25, 1940, President Roosevelt explained to the American public the need for the United States to prepare for the possibility of war and stated that the government would be budgeting substantial funds for expansion of military production and facilities. By the time that Roosevelt visited Newport on August 12, 1940, as a part of his inspection tour of military facilities in New England, work and planning for the development of new naval activities was underway. Arriving aboard the presidential yacht, USS *Potomac*, the president, Secretary of the Navy Frank Knox, Rhode Island governor William Henry Vanderbilt III, U.S. senator Theodore F. Green of Rhode Island, Newport mayor Henry S. Wheeler, members of Congress from the New England area and local military leaders led by Admiral Edward C. Kalbfus, president of the Naval War College, took part in the inspection.

In 1940 and early 1941, naval activities in Narragansett Bay lacked the command structure and infrastructure to support the planned expansion. Various commands had their own chains of command and did not report to anyone locally. The creation and expansion of naval facilities around the bay, primarily on Conanicut Island and at Quonset Point and Davisville, resulted in more new naval commands. With the increased need for coordination becoming evident, it was determined that a flag officer should be placed in charge of all naval activities in Narragansett Bay. On April 1, 1941, Naval Operating Base Newport (NOB Newport) for all U.S. Navy activities in and around Narragansett Bay was established with the president of the Naval War College, then Admiral Kalbfus, as its commandant. Naval

Aerial view of a portion of Coddington Point, showing wooden barracks and classrooms for the Naval Training Station, September 1944. *Naval War College Museum Collections.*

reserve units in Fall River, New Bedford, Newport, Pawtucket, Woonsocket and Providence also came under the base command for coordination of activities. On Aquidneck Island alone, it was necessary to purchase two thousand acres of land to create this command infrastructure.

Under Kalbfus's leadership, the great buildup within Narragansett Bay began. Although he served as commandant only until November 2, 1942, he oversaw significant changes, such as the creation of a supply depot, a net depot, a PT boat base and training facility at Melville, fuel storage tanks, ammunition storage facilities, increased housing units, new roads that would change the traffic patterns around Aquidneck Island, the Naval Air Station at Quonset Point, the Naval Construction Training Center at Davisville and numerous other support facilities.

Once the United States declared war on Japan and Germany in December 1941, activity in Newport, Aquidneck Island and Narragansett Bay accelerated. During the expansion of the U.S. Navy during the period from July 1940 through July 1943, it built 333 combat ships, 1,274 minesweepers and patrol craft, 151 auxiliary vessels and 12,964 landing craft. No country in history had ever engaged in such an ambitious naval construction program.

The mission for the Naval Training Station during World War II was focused on training and educating naval personnel, whether officers or enlisted men, to man both new and existing navy warships. Training sought to bridge the gap for recruits from civilian to military life, introducing them to discipline, naval duties and esprit de corps, as well as educating them in technical matters and in general preparing them as thoroughly and expeditiously as possible for duty in the fleet. The length of the training period depended on the course. For example, the general line course for officers was eight weeks. Navigation training took four

Naval trainees in the Pre-Commissioning School at the Naval Training Station. *Naval War College Museum Collections.*

weeks, while Diesel School lasted eight weeks and the course for hospital corpsmen took six weeks.

In prewar years at the Training Station, 700 to 800 men per month went through boot camp. By November 1941, that number had increased to 2,800. Following the attack on Pearl Harbor, the number of recruits at the Training Station rose to 8,600 per month. In total, during World War II, an astounding 204,115 recruits were trained at NTS Newport.

To accommodate the influx of men for the training, a massive construction project ensued—extending onto the Coddington Point side of the base—adding more barracks and Quonset huts, instructional and administrative buildings, base fire and police buildings, medical buildings and a new Naval Supply Depot building. Construction contracts for $10 million resulted in the Training Station reaching a housing capacity for twenty-two thousand trainees.

In January 1944, the Training Station went in a different direction, ceasing its training of individual recruits and creating a new program known as pre-commissioning training, which involved training the crew of each large combat ship at one time. In all, an average of 85 percent of a ship's crew would meet in Newport to start training, attending such schools as firefighting, damage control, gunnery, cargo handling and engineering. During the pre-commissioning program, which ran from November 1943 until December 21, 1946, more than 300,000 sailors passed through the Training Station on their way to the newest ships in the navy. They were assisted by the cruisers *Augusta* and *Savannah*. For example, on April 22, 1945, *Augusta* arrived at Newport and took 11 officers and 300 men designated for the new cruiser USS *Columbus* on a five-day training cruise.

The validity of this new program was established with the first ship to receive this training, USS *Franklin* (CV-13), an Essex-class aircraft carrier commissioned on January 31, 1944. By June 1944, the massive carrier was launching its first warplanes, supporting the invasion of the Marianas in the Pacific. On the morning of October 30, three enemy bombers attempted to crash into the carrier while it was while supporting landing and action around Leyte. One hit *Franklin*'s starboard side, the second hit the flight deck and crashed through to the gallery deck (killing fifty-six and wounding sixty) and the third was a near miss. After a two-month battle damage overhaul in Seattle, *Franklin* returned to action and by March 18 was launching airstrikes against the Japanese homeland. Before dawn on March 19, an enemy plane dropped two semi–armor piercing bombs that hit the carrier. One struck the flight deck and penetrated to the hangar deck, igniting fires. The second tore through two decks and started raging fires that, in turn, ignited ammunition,

Naval trainees muster in preparation for leaving the Naval Training Station for assignment to a single ship, circa 1944. *Naval War College Museum Collections.*

bombs and rockets. *Franklin* was soon without power, with a thirteen-degree list, all within only fifty miles of the Japanese mainland. Casualties totaled 807 killed and 487 wounded. After evacuating the seriously wounded, a total of 106 officers and 604 enlisted men remained with the ship. Through their valiant efforts—and assistance from the USS *Santa Fe*—they were able to save the ship. The training these men received in Newport no doubt helped them contain the fires and keep the carrier afloat.

As the Naval Training Station reached its capacity for expansion, facilities were built at other places around Aquidneck Island. At Price's Neck on Newport's Ocean Drive, an Anti-Aircraft Training Center was established on over 26 acres, and eighty-nine buildings were constructed there. There were twenty-nine antiaircraft guns and even a tilting platform to simulate the pitch and roll that would be experienced on board a ship. During the war, the December 7, 1945 edition of the *Newport Mercury* reported, "The night skies off the city filled with streamers of tracer bullets, the days with the puffs of exploding shells. The air, day and night, resounded with the bark of the guns and the rattle of the shells." For the site of a new Naval Rifle Range, 165 acres at Sachuest Point in Middletown were purchased for the building of eight ranges, barracks for seven hundred men and other support buildings. Later, the receiver site for the Naval Communication Station Newport was established at Sachuest Point.

Between 1941 and 1944, the Bureau of Yards and Docks spent a total of $85,242,000 in the Newport area. Of that amount, over $25 million was devoted to improving the inadequate facilities of the Torpedo Station. On Goat Island, that meant new buildings for storage, assembling, training and administration. The power plant was expanded to meet the increase in power requirements. Pier facilities for docking and loading were expanded, and a new ferry slip was constructed. All of this construction led to the need to reclaim land on the north end of the island, but alas, there was not enough area on Goat Island. So, the Torpedo Station expanded into Middletown. Forty-nine buildings, a ferry slip, a spur off the main line of the New York, New Haven and Hartford Railroad and multiple roads to connect all of the buildings were built. This new infrastructure allowed for a

Aerial view of naval facilities at Coddington Cove, including Torpedo Station Annex No. 1, and, at the far right, the marine barracks, in July 1945. *Naval War College Museum Collections*.

major portion of the research, design and torpedo equipment department, as well as the central office, to be transferred from Goat Island. The 205-acre property became known as Annex No. 1.

In February 1942, dredging and construction began on the new buildings on the northern end of Gould Island, which grew into the overhaul and testing facility for torpedoes in the area. The island was dominated by the large brick building that served as the overhaul shop and the long passage to the firing pier on the north end of the island. The torpedo range ran to the north approximately six miles, passing between Prudence and Hope Islands. The facility was completed in 1943 and designed for proof-firing one hundred torpedoes per day. It would test fire seventy-five thousand torpedoes during the war.

Both Prudence Island and Hope Island were used for weapons storage facilities. The southern tip of Prudence Island, part of the town of Portsmouth, was purchased as a site of a naval magazine for the storage of ammunition. Few in the area even knew of its existence. In addition to the twenty-five magazines located there, facilities were built to support assigned personnel. Housing consisted of barracks for 224 men, married and bachelor officer quarters, a mess hall and a recreational building. To ensure fresh water, a fifty-thousand-gallon concrete reservoir was placed underground. Additionally, to facilitate loading and offloading, a five-hundred-foot T-shaped pier was built extending to the south.

During World War II, the Naval Fuel Depot at Melville was determined to be inadequate to meet anticipated demands and, therefore, was expanded to become part of the defense fuel support point, which extended south along Defense Highway, which ran along the western side of Aquidneck Island. Construction began immediately to build seven steel and four concrete oil tanks with a capacity of twenty-seven thousand barrels, in addition to thirty-four prestressed concrete oil tanks, each with a capacity for sixty thousand barrels.

The second, and possibly the most recognized use of the Melville property, was as the training site for the Motor Torpedo Boat Squadrons Training Center. Housing for this base was in the form of 154 Quonset huts. There were also 7 metal buildings used as shops for repair and instruction and a wood-framed building for instruction.

The Melville facility's third use was the location of the Naval Net Depot, necessitating the construction of two large storehouses and one large concrete slab for the repair of antisubmarine nets. This facility supported the use of antisubmarine nets and electronic mines across the East and West

Aerial view of the Anti-Aircraft Training Center at Price's Neck on Brenton Point during the war. Jerry Browe informed Christian McBurney that as a teenager he lived near Price's Neck and heard day and night the "rat tat tat" of the guns and saw streams of bright tracers piercing the night sky. *Naval War College Museum Collections*.

Passages of Narragansett Bay, to prevent enemy submarines or other craft from entering the bay.

It was determined that new defensive installations were necessary to protect Newport. There were three 5-inch director-operated navy-type guns and four 90-millimeter director-operated army guns (mobile equipment) at two sites: at the intersection of Eustis Avenue and Bliss Road and near Ruggles Avenue. These sites had reinforced-concrete emplacements, steel igloo-style surface magazines, underground concrete ammunition magazines and housing, mess and sanitation facilities. Other gun emplacements were positioned around the other islands in the bay. Rose Island, Gould Island, Conanicut Island and Coasters Harbor Island all had gun batteries under the purview of the U.S. Army.

During World War II, more than one hundred aircraft carriers, battleships, cruisers, destroyers and other naval vessels moved in and out of Narragansett Bay. To accommodate these ships, there were thirty-one mooring buoys in the bay, from Jamestown to Melville. In total, taking into account the peak numbers of navy personnel, an estimated 162,823 officers, sailors and navy-associated civilians served in Rhode Island at one time (see Appendix B).

Importantly, all of this growth required the expansion of public utilities to ensure uninterrupted electrical power. This was accomplished by establishing an easement for electrical power by constructing an electrical transmission system that could be clamped to the Mount Hope Bridge. This allowed a 660-kilovolt line to run from the Warren substation to the north end of the navy property at Melville where it would be stepped down to 22 kilovolts and fed into the electrical system that interconnected nearly all of the naval activities in the Newport area.

The facilities for water supply also needed attention. In 1941, the demand for water was at three million gallons per day and by 1943 had increased to four million gallons per day. This issue was solved by the development of a dam, a water treatment plant and a filtered water reservoir in Lawton Valley in Portsmouth. Additionally, water lines were run from Nonquit Pond in Tiverton to St. Mary's Reservoir in Portsmouth.

Housing the tremendous influx of naval and governmental workers—and sometimes their families—was a goal that was sought throughout the war years but never adequately achieved. In 1940, with the purchase of the land to develop what was named the Anchorage, housing increased for naval personnel by 600 units (150 houses, each with 4 units). Castlewood, a Renaissance- and Louis XV–style mansion located at Maple Avenue and Girard Avenue outside of the Maple Street exit (Gate 4) was taken over and opened as Miantonomi Hall on January 15, 1943. It was later demolished as a part of a public housing project for Torpedo Station workers. With the drawdown of workers at the Torpedo Station, the housing was then opened for junior enlisted personnel. It was later subsumed into the Tonomy Hill low-income housing project that was part of the response by the Federal Housing Authority. (The FHA constructed several projects: Tonomy Hill, Dexter Place and the Perry Mill Dormitory.) The Newport Housing Authority contributed with the Park Holm project. All of this development occurred during the war years.

On base, housing, feeding and clothing the increased numbers became the dominant problem. New barracks, drill halls and recreational facilities, as well as numerous provision and general storehouses were built. Even with all of these efforts, the housing shortage remained critical throughout the war and contributed to substandard housing being offered at premium rental prices.

The expansion of naval facilities in the Narragansett Bay area quickly taxed the capabilities and resources offered at the Naval Hospital at

Newport. By 1940, a major infusion of funding was required. The result was the erection of 9 new emergency wards that increased capacity by 468 beds. New housing provided accommodations for 46 nurses and a new barracks for hospital corpsmen provided housing, cafeteria and recreational facilities. All of this construction required the acquisition of land north of the hospital up to Training Station Road and new concrete roadways connecting the new buildings.

More than five hundred marines protected the various navy facilities in Narragansett Bay. At Coddington Point, at the Torpedo Station Annex, a new marine barracks was constructed.

One facility that did not expand during the war was the Naval War College. Still, it remained open, although courses were abbreviated and the curriculum emphasized a new command course and a preparatory staff course. In the 1920s and '30s, many of the top admirals participated in war

The cruiser USS *Savannah* is inspected at Newport in May 1945, when it served as a school ship for pre-commissioned crews. On September 11, 1943, it suffered serious damage from a German radio-controlled glide bomb. While courageously supervising rescue operations after the attack and refusing to leave his post, Lieutenant John J. Kirwin of Newport died from smoke inhalation. *Harry S. Truman Library.*

games against Japan at the War College. After the war, Admiral Chester Nimitz stated:

The war with Japan had been reenacted in the game room [at the War College] *by so many people and in so many ways that nothing that happened during the war was a surprise—absolutely nothing except the Kamikaze tactics toward the end of the war.*

Even the three-masted training ship, USS *Constellation*, which was thought to have been built in 1797 and in use during the War of 1812 (but was later determined to have been constructed in 1854) and had served as a training ship in Newport since 1894, served as overflow barracks during the war. In addition, it was designated as the relief (or standby) flagship for the Atlantic Fleet, and the flag was shifted from the heavy cruiser USS *Augusta* to it from January 19 to July 20, 1942. Vice Admiral Royal E. Ingersoll transferred his staff and three-star flag from the heavy cruiser USS *Augusta* after he had received word that the German battleship *Tirpitz* had slipped out into the Atlantic Ocean. Ingersoll wanted *Augusta* to steam out of Newport and join in the chase for the German battleship without the burden of also serving as the flagship. After departing *Constellation* in July, Ingersoll told a news reporter, "Personally, I have never had a more enjoyable time on any ship." *Constellation* again served as the flagship during 1943 and 1944.

The United Service Organization, or USO, was created in 1941 through a mandate from President Roosevelt challenging six organizations to create venues to meet the recreational needs of servicemen and women while they were on leave. Those six organizations—the Salvation Army, the National Jewish Welfare Board, YMCA, YWCA, the National Catholic Community Service and the Travelers Aid Association—met the challenge. On March 1, 1942, a new USO club was dedicated on Commercial Wharf in Newport. Thought to be the largest USO club in the nation at the time, there was an eight-hundred-seat auditorium on the second level, in addition to locker and shower rooms and apartments for members of the staff. The third floor was a dormitory set up with bunk beds and lockers. Other USO clubs were opened in Jamestown and East Greenwich. In early 1944, at what is now 28 Marcus Wheatland Boulevard, a USO recreation center was constructed for servicemen of color. During the war, black men were permitted to serve on board large warships only as cooks and stewards, but they had expanded roles on smaller vessels and on shore, including as Seabees.

The Navy Department also leased the second deck of the Casino on Bellevue Avenue as club facilities for naval officers. Another establishment was the Robinson House, known as Heartsease, on the corner of Kay and Ayrault Streets. Within the three-story mansion were a library, a ballroom, a game room, a dining room, a dormitory and bedrooms.

The increased number of ships and naval personnel arriving in Narragansett Bay necessitated the expansion of facilities around Government Landing. Acquiring the waterfront property of the Old Colony Railroad in 1941, the navy began an extensive building program to include barracks, a mess hall, administrative buildings, guard houses and heating plants. The building program continued and ultimately included a new ferry slip to support activities on Goat and Gould Islands, a large shore patrol headquarters to support the local police, a post office and facilities for the Coast Guard and small craft maintenance.

In summary, the period from 1939 to 1945 was one of great growth by the military in Narragansett Bay and on Aquidneck Island in particular. Some of the land taken for defense purposes during World War II (often through condemnation proceedings) was returned to the original owners or declared excess by the government and returned to state, local or civilian use. The process continues to this day, as the navy disposes of various land parcels around Aquidneck Island as a part of the Base Realignment and Closure (BRAC) process. Most of this land was acquired by the navy during World II.

7

Liberty Ships and More

CIVILIAN WORKERS AND MANUFACTURERS BOLSTER THE WAR EFFORT

By Patrick T. Conley

In December 1941, when the global war finally engulfed America, tiny Rhode Island was still an industrial giant despite the slow, insidious southward movement of textile production, its major manufacturing enterprise. Of the state's 1940 population of 713,000, some 92,000 joined the military, with nearly 2,200 losing their lives in the war. Nonetheless, a substantial workforce remained, swelled by the entry of women into Rhode Island defense plants. Those civilians made an enormous contribution to America's war effort, although a less dramatic or hazardous one than that of actual combatants. As in World War I, America again became the "arsenal of democracy."

Construction of naval bases occupied great numbers of civilian workers. Nearly eleven thousand made the huge Naval Air Station at Quonset Point and helped to build adjacent Camp Endicott at Davisville, home of the Seabees and the famed Naval Construction Training Center. Some three thousand workers at Davisville also produced more than thirty-two thousand Quonset huts for shipment around the world.

Rhode Island civilians also aided in the construction of Naval Auxiliary Airfields in Westerly and Charlestown. They further expanded the Torpedo Station at Newport and the Naval Fuel Depot at Melville in addition to building the Motor Torpedo Boat Squadrons Training Center in Melville. And they built numerous coastal fortifications, especially in Jamestown, Little Compton, Narragansett and various

"W.J. Halloran, Providence, R.I., relies on Autocar heavy-duty trucks to deliver Quonset Huts on time." From an advertisement in *Life* magazine, June 12, 1944. *Courtesy of Autocar, LLC, © Autocar, LLC.*

islands in Narragansett Bay. Their sheer number and cost (some $130 million) prompted the federal government in April 1942 to declare Rhode Island's coast a military district.

In Newport, the Torpedo Station on Goat Island employed some thirteen thousand people in the production of these lethal weapons. Extra housing had to be built in and near Newport to accommodate the thousands of men trained at the expanded Naval Training Station near the Naval War College.

Meanwhile, private industry did its part. The war was the "last hurrah" for Rhode Island's textile companies. In the Blackstone, Pawtuxet and Woonasquatucket Valleys, cotton, wool and rayon mills loomed large in the war effort, producing great numbers of uniforms, blankets, parachutes, gas masks, field jackets and other combat gear. The jewelry industry, which was hurt by being unable to use silver for nonmilitary purposes, still made a salutary contribution by fashioning insignia and buttons for military uniforms, as well as medals, with female workers primarily doing the careful work.

During World War II, world-famous silverware manufacturer Gorham Manufacturing Company, based in Providence, virtually abandoned its civilian industries to focus on producing goods for the war effort. These included small arms parts, tank bearings, torpedo components and millions of 40-millimeter shell casings. Yale University Art Gallery has in its collections a World War II "machine gun" munitions factory medal Gorham made in 1945.

Rhode Island's once huge metals and machinery industry literally retooled and proved to be especially significant. Machine tools were vital to war production at the nation's factories—the tools made assembly of airplanes, tanks and other weapons possible. Its giant, Brown & Sharpe, nearly doubled its workforce to eleven thousand during the war to craft an array of metal machine tools and precision instruments for military uses. In 1942, Brown & Sharpe's open-shop policy, perhaps the oldest in U.S. industry at the time, was swept aside when the National War Labor Board awarded the International Association of Machinists a contract after an election in which a substantial majority of the firm's employees chose this union to represent them.

Elsewhere in Providence, the Federal Products Company made gauges, and the Imperial Knife Company furnished blades and bayonets. In Cranston, Universal Winding Company set up a new firm, the Cranston Arms Company, to manufacture Johnson semiautomatic rifles and machine guns for the Marine Corps and the Dutch army, while Fireside Builders Products Corporation, formerly a steel fabricating plant, employed over one thousand workers crafting masts for American warships and pontoons for emergency wharfs, bridges and dry docks.

Invented by Antoine Gazda, an Austrian immigrant who worked secretly out of the Biltmore Hotel in Providence, the 20-millimeter Oerlikon-Gazda antiaircraft gun was installed aboard most U.S. Navy warships, from PT boats to battleships. Gazda parts were made in machine shops around the Blackstone Valley, including at Woonsocket's Taft-Pierce Manufacturing Company (employing some two thousand workers); Pawtucket's Pantex Pressing Machine Company; Lincoln Machine Company; and Providence's Liberty Tool & Gauge Company. About twenty-six thousand of the famous guns were assembled at a converted textile mill, the Manville-Jenckes factory in Pawtucket.

The state's rubber factories, the youngest of its Big Five industries, contributed over fifty different products from U.S. Rubber Company plants in Providence and Bristol. The Davol Corporation in Providence manufactured an array of medical supplies. In Woonsocket, the dormant Alice Mill, founded by Rhode Island's legendary "Rubber King," Joseph Banigan, bounced back to produce inflatable boats, wading suits and balloons for convoy use. In a top-secret endeavor, Woonsocket rubber workers produced one of the war's most unusual creations—inflatable tanks and other military weapons for General Patton's decoy army, a fictitious force designed to deceive Germany (as it did, successfully) regarding the exact site of the June 1944 Allied invasion of France. "It was all hush-hush, everybody was supposed to keep quiet," recalled Del Gariepy of Woonsocket, one of the 1,500 workers at the factory—and they did. Truly, Rhode Island's many manufacturers and their skilled millhands waged war on the homefront.

Of course, Rhode Island's workers and its shipyards excelled at making boats and ships for the U.S. Navy. During World War II, five different shipyards were kept busy on military and merchant marine contracts. Four of the smaller yards specialized in wooden-hulled boats, a skill that had almost disappeared except for yachts and fishing trawlers.

In Bristol, the world-famous Herreshoff Manufacturing Company, then directed by Carl W. Haffenreffer, transitioned from crafting the finest racing yachts to the construction of one hundred small wooden-hulled naval craft for the navy from October 1942 into 1945. The company built, in order of length, two 130-foot minesweepers called YMSs; twenty-two 103-foot-long coastal transports, known as APcs; four 97-foot coastal minesweepers known as AMcs; eight 85-foot army rescue vessels; twenty 71-foot PT boats (all of which were sent in 1944 to the U.S.'s then ally the Soviet Union); eight 71-foot British Vosper PT boats; and thirty-six 63-foot army/navy air-sea rescue boats. After successful launchings, Haffenreffer treated his workers with rounds of beer from his family's Narragansett Brewery. (One of the YMSs launched at Bristol was sunk by a mine off the Pacific island of Palau in 1944.)

Anchorage Incorporated operated a small shipyard in Warren (the Warren Boat Yard), building six coastal transports (APcs), four of which were sent to the British Royal Navy. From 1942 to 1944, in Wickford, a shipyard operated by Perkins & Vaughan completed nine 110-foot submarine chasers for the U.S. Navy, and a shipyard run by Harris and Parsons at nearby East Greenwich constructed eight more of the same vessel. These vessels were armed with a 75-millimeter cannon, three 20-millimeter cannons, depth charges and hedgehogs. Three of the submarine chasers constructed at each shipyard were sent to the Soviet Union in early 1945. In 1945, each shipyard built three 72-foot harbor defense motor launches (HDMLs) for the Royal Navy. These projects

One of twenty-two coastal transports known as APcs built by the Herreshoff Manufacturing Company at Bristol from October 1942 to July 1943—an average of nearly one a week. *Courtesy of Halsey C. Herreshoff and the Herreshoff Marine Museum.*

Herreshoff Manufacturing Company workers construct warships at the Bristol shipyard during the war. *Courtesy of Halsey C. Herreshoff and the Herreshoff Marine Museum.*

brought jobs—for example, at the East Greenwich shipyard, the number of workers increased from 15 to 185.

Rhode Island's most prodigious civilian effort was the building of sixty-four large combat vessels at the Providence Shipyard from March 1942 through mid-1945 by a civilian workforce that peaked at 21,264 in January 1945. No other manufacturing project in Rhode Island history achieved this scale of participation.

In the weeks after Pearl Harbor, the U.S. Maritime Commission selected the Port of Providence as a construction site, initially for the famous Liberty ships. Vice Admiral Howard Vickery, who directed this effort for the Maritime Commission, decided in March 1942 that the Providence facility should have six shipways (onto which a huge keel was laid and hulls were constructed for each vessel) and that the Rheem Manufacturing Company, experienced in making water heaters (but not boats), should develop the shipyard. Unlike most other port cities, Providence was at a distinct disadvantage because it lacked an existing shipyard. It not only had to build one but also train a workforce.

Rheem struggled from the outset, not only because of inexperience in shipbuilding but also because of the daunting task of quickly converting the pastoral public park at Field's Point into an efficient 144-acre manufacturing facility. The site, hilly on the northern end with mudflats on the south, proved difficult to develop. Unfortunately, Fort Independence, a hilltop Revolutionary War breastwork, was leveled in the process—as were a number of hilltop residences in the Washington Park neighborhood—in order to create parking and provide fill for the mudflats. These problems had not yet been solved when Rheem was ousted on February 28, 1943, in favor of the Walsh-Kaiser Company Incorporated. Its inauspicious start gave the Providence enterprise the slowest average production time for Liberty ships of the eighteen yards that built them.

From its original contract for thirty-two Liberty ships, Rheem launched only two: the *William Coddington* in late November 1942, named in honor of Newport's founder, and the *John Clarke* on February 25, 1943, dedicated to the Newport physician and Baptist clergyman who procured Rhode Island's famed Royal Charter of 1663. The *Clarke* was launched stern-first—like all the others—just three days before Walsh-Kaiser Company assumed management of the shipyard, but it was not delivered to the navy until April 12. Walsh-Kaiser took credit for the *Clarke* because it "delivered" the vessel to the navy, but the count should be as follows: Rheem, two Liberty-class vessels; Walsh-Kaiser, nine Liberty ships, twenty-one frigates and thirty-two combat-loaded cargo ships. Rheem laid the keels of four of the Liberty ships later completed by Walsh-Kaiser: the *Samuel Gorton*, the *James DeWolfe*, the *Lyman Abbott* (named for a Massachusetts man) and the *Moses Brown*. The irony of naming successive Liberty ships for a notorious Rhode Island slave trader (DeWolfe) and an ardent abolitionist (Brown) completely escaped those in charge of the dedication process.

The eleven Liberty-class ships produced in Providence were blunt-nosed, flat-bottomed freighters, designed for a crew of eighty hands—forty-four merchant seamen and thirty-six naval armed guards to man the deck guns. Each hull had a full-length inner bottom to maximize carrying capacity while accommodating fuel oil, water, ballast tanks and a huge three-cylinder oil-fired steam reciprocating engine. They were approximately 442 feet in length, with a 58-foot beam. "Liberties," as they were sometimes called, had a fully loaded draft of more than 27 feet, displaced 14,100 tons, weighed 10,500 tons and were propelled by a single screw to reach a cruising speed of a mere eleven knots.

These cargo vessels carried not only small planes but also tanks, trucks, jeeps, fuel and ammunition. Some eventually became troop transports as well. Their cost to build ranged from $1.5 to $2.1 million each.

Most sobering is that 733 cargo ships—including 196 Liberties—operated by the U.S. Merchant Marine, were sunk with a loss of over 7,000 lives, according to the final report of the federal War Shipping Administration. Of these fatalities, 5,638 were merchant sailors, who had a casualty rate of 1 mariner for every 32 who served. This death rate exceeded that of the army and the navy and was close to that of the Marine Corps. As a number of historians have observed, the United States achieved a goal of building merchant ships faster than the Germans and Japanese could sink them.

In defense of Providence's first great government contractor, inexperience and topography were not its only obstacles to success. On December 31, 1942, the shipyard suffered Rhode Island's single costliest fire. Just after two o'clock in the afternoon, workers at the fabrication plant noticed smoke billowing from the pump house at the east wall of the huge building (643 feet long, 255 feet wide). In the plant at that time were several hundred workers cutting steel plates for the four Liberty ships then under construction. The 156,000-square-foot structure had been sheathed in plywood because of the unavailability of sheet metal. Flames vaulted the east wall, and within minutes the fire was out of control. Workers ran for their lives.

Complicating the task for firefighters, the sprinkler equipment—which had arrived five months earlier—had not yet been installed. Before 3:00 p.m., more than thirty pieces of fire apparatus from Providence and adjacent Cranston were battling the blaze, while members of twelve auxiliary fire companies were on standby. Within an hour, all that remained of the huge building was its steel framework. The loss was later estimated at $1.7 million (in 1942 dollars), including valuable production equipment. Fortunately, no one was seriously injured.

Walsh-Kaiser, the Providence Shipyard's second manager and contractor, hit the ground running when on February 28, 1943, it assumed the shipbuilding contract, along with 11,189 employees. The firm had evolved from a joint venture between Iowa-based contractor Thomas J. Walsh and prominent West Coast shipbuilder Henry J. Kaiser. Supervising numerous large-scale wartime projects, Kaiser immediately sent some sixteen top executives from his California shipyards to improve the organization at the Providence Shipyard. They left after a few months, and for the rest of the war the shipbuilding efforts were led by the Walsh Company. Walsh, impressively, had built the Queens–Midtown Tunnel under the East River to New York City and two of the largest dry docks in the world, including one at the Brooklyn Navy Yard. But it lacked experience constructing ships. Walsh's employees were placed under the able direction of Jack Macdonald, who acted as the project's general manager until the war's end.

By September 1943, the construction expertise of the Walsh Company resolved the site problems that had vexed Rheem, and Kaiser's shipbuilding know-how put the reduced Liberty ship production schedule on an even keel. For one, playing to its strong suit, Walsh fixed the muddy, water-logged site left by Rheem, building roads, raising floors and keeping work areas dry. Labor relations also improved. One executive stated that while Rheem had a union contract, "at lunch hour they allowed three different labor organizations to make speeches, and the result was a little fistfight on the fringe of the crowd and they talked it over all afternoon." When the Walsh-Kaiser joint venture took over, the American Federation of Labor (AFL) was the sole union at the site. One Walsh executive gushed in early 1944, "I don't think there is an organization in any way that has had 18,000 men that has had less labor trouble that we have had." Workers started out earning $0.92 an hour and with some experience could move up to $1.28 per hour, a wage rate significantly higher than other industries.

When in full operation, the 144-acre Providence Shipyard included such structures as administrative offices; a Marine Corps inspection station; a plate shop; an assembly shop; electric, machine, pipe and sheet-metal shops; a warehouse; subcontractor facilities; two outfitting piers; and six shipways.

Encouraged by the yard's projected transformation, the Maritime Commission soon awarded Walsh-Kaiser a contract for the construction of twenty-one submarine-fighting frigates, the largest allocation of these vessels made to any American shipyard. In an amazing display of smooth-functioning mass production, all of these frigates cleared the ways between July 14 and November 21, 1943.

Walsh-Kaiser's portion of the ninety-six frigates built nationwide was assigned to Great Britain, thereby receiving the Royal Navy's designation of HMS. These twin-screw, 304-foot-long ships with 37-foot beams had two reciprocal four-cylinder triple-expansion engines powered by steam (made by Vickers in Canada) that propelled them at a speed of twenty knots. Each one carried a crew of 143 men. Their small size belied their complexity, as they were equipped with guns, depth charges, gear for underwater detection and radar. They were intended and designed by Kaiser's Oakland, California plant as fighting chaperones for Allied merchant fleets.

In May 1943, with production in full swing, the U.S. Navy gave a new and huge chore to the Providence Shipyard: the construction of thirty-two combat-loaded cargo vessels. These newly designed ships (also called auxiliary attack cargo ships, or AKAs), at 426 feet, were nearly as long as the Liberty ships, with approximately the same beam (58 feet), but they were faster (eighteen knots), much more complex and more difficult to build. Importantly, each one had to meet combat-ready specifications set by the U.S. Navy, including being heavily armored. There was 75 percent more welding on a combat cargo ship than on a Liberty ship. The twin-screw AKAs, powered by two turbo-electric engines, were designed to carry both crew (280 men) and troops (267 soldiers). They were equipped with the latest detection devices and housed three radio rooms, three radar stations and two engine rooms. Conveniences included a barbershop, a laundry, a tailor shop, a huge galley, a hospital and a dental office.

The first AKA, USS *Artemis*, was named for a star, as were all its successors. *Artemis* had its keel laid on November 23, 1943, and was launched 280 days later on May 20, 1944. It took 2,267,000 man hours to build this first AKA, at a cost of $3,803,560. Thereafter, the yard's pace quickened dramatically because of prefabrication and assembly line techniques. By the fourteenth one, it took just 798,676 man hours, at a cost of $2,052,269. Under contract to deliver thirty-two AKAs, Walsh-Kaiser averaged just 136 days from keel laying to delivery. One of these intricate ships, then the latest word in amphibious warfare, left the shipyard about every ten days for a period of more than ten months until the USS *Zenobia* took its 605-foot slide down one of the yard's six ways on July 6, 1945. Most of these AKAs passed through the Panama Canal and supported amphibious landings and other action against Japan in the Pacific.

The *Artemis*, the first combat-loaded cargo vessel, being built on a way at Providence's Walsh-Kaiser shipyard, in early 1944. *Andresen, Providence Shipyard.*

Thus, at one point, the Providence Shipyard had four different programs all proceeding at once, which understandably created some inefficiencies. The first program was for six Liberties; the second was for the twenty-one frigates; the third was for six more Liberties (one was canceled); and the fourth program was for thirty-two combat-ready cargo ships.

Sign at the entrance to the Walsh-Kaiser Shipyard exhorting workers to build ten more combat-loaded cargo ships in 1944. *Andresen, Providence Shipyard*.

While women made up a larger proportion of the workplace at companies like Brown & Sharpe and Gorham Manufacturing than at the Walsh-Kaiser shipyard, women were an integral part of the productive population at Field's Point. Of the nearly three thousand women employed at the shipyard, 60 percent had actual production (rather than clerical) jobs. These women did the same work and received the same pay as men because all workers, excluding those at the executive and professional levels, were members of the American Federation of Labor. "Rosie the Riveter" was more than a slogan or a symbol at Field's Point; she was a shipbuilder.

For the shipyard's operatives, it was not all work and no play. Social activities and special events were frequent. Workers doubled as entertainers and even formed a talented shipyard orchestra. They held blood drives, memorial ceremonies and patriotic observances, and their war bond rallies raised nearly $14 million. Walsh-Kaiser fielded baseball, softball, football and basketball squads to compete with local teams and those of other industries, and it won a New England industrial-league baseball championship in 1943. Employees also published an eight-page weekly newspaper, the *Yardarm*, featuring local and plant news.

Rhode Island wartime governor J. Howard McGrath took an active and personal interest in shipyard activities throughout the war. In late October 1944, he brought his friend, Harry S. Truman, then appearing in Providence to campaign for a fourth term for Franklin Roosevelt as president and for himself as vice president, to view the shipyard and to thank the workers for their "noble efforts." In September 1945, President Truman appointed McGrath his solicitor general. Another strong shipyard supporter was Providence mayor Dennis J. Roberts, who doubled as a lieutenant commander in the U.S. Naval Reserve during the war. He made sure that extra housing was built near the shipyard and that trolleys were able to transport workers efficiently from Downtown to Field's Point.

Occasionally, Walsh-Kaiser would hear about the performance of its ships. Harold J. Gregory, master of the *Jesse H. Metcalf*, named for a prominent Rhode Island senator of the time, wrote in an October 5, 1944 letter:

> *Since leaving your yard, she has steamed 11,700 miles, under varying conditions of weather and loading....We have encountered seas heavy enough to cause her to roll thirty-five degrees each way....Through fair weather and foul, we have steamed along with or ahead of the rest of them, and there has been no sign of failure in machinery, hull or rigging. To say that I am proud of her is putting it mildly.*

Several of the ships produced in Rhode Island were sunk, either in combat or in accidents. The USS *Stephen Hopkins* actually sank a German commerce raider on September 27, 1942, using its lone four-inch gun after an hours-long gun battle. This Liberty ship was the only U.S. warship to sink a German surface ship in World War II. But the Providence-made ship sank as well, and the surviving crew of fifteen made a month-long two-thousand-mile lifeboat voyage to safety in Brazil.

It is said that "all good [and great] things must end," and so it was with Providence's shipyard. A sharp decline in the workforce occurred during 1945, as the war's imminent conclusion became both more apparent, and the various departments completed their final contractual assignments. The shipyard soon closed and was sold to the City of Providence in December 1945 for $308,093.08. (After the federal government had ploughed more than $10 million into it.) It was then sold to a private developer in 1949. Thereafter the word *shipyard* was affixed to a few of the business ventures that occupied the spacious site, most notably the Shipyard Drive-In and the Shipyard Ten-Pin Bowling Lanes. These businesses were relatively short-lived, like the shipyard itself. Today, only the memories of it linger on in the minds of those relatively few survivors of Rhode Island's greatest ever industrial enterprise.

8

Women at Work Outside the Home

By Christian McBurney

Before World War II, men and women employed outside the home worked at vastly different jobs. For example, in the 1930s, 84 percent of insurance companies and 65 percent of banks would not hire married women. School committees routinely fired female teachers when they married or became pregnant. Women did lower-paying clerical work, worked on the lower scale in a factory or worked as domestics in other people's homes. The Great Depression, which ravaged the country during the 1930s, made matters worse.

The Japanese raid on Pearl Harbor and America's subsequent role in fighting on the Allied side in World War II changed all that. Many of the state's young men volunteered to join the army, navy, marines or merchant marine. The involuntary draft came soon afterward. In Rhode Island, women by the thousands were needed to fill the jobs left behind in manufacturing plants, most of which had been converted to making materiel and weapons supporting the war effort. New or enlarged military bases gave rise to a demand for clerical and other white-collar work.

Women met this increase in demand, joining the workforce outside the home in droves. Many of them were the wives of servicemen, effectively taking their places at factories. Others were the wives or children of farmers or millhands.

Of course, many women during the war performed the traditional and important role of caring for children and elderly family members, which had been the lot of adult women for generations. Even here, work changed.

Many stay-at-home mothers helped neighbors working outside the home by looking after their children or elders, and they made the best of rationing and grew vegetables in their victory gardens. But this chapter focuses on the changing landscape of the workforce for women outside the home.

Some Rhode Island women contributed to the war effort in direct ways, by volunteering to serve as nurses or in other posts in the U.S. Army with the WACs (Women's Army Corps), in the U.S. Naval Reserve's WAVES (Women Accepted for Volunteer Emergency Service) or with the U.S. Coast Guard's SPARs (*Semper Paratus*, or Always Ready). Most of these women served outside Rhode Island, including overseas or at hospitals on nearby Cape Cod that cared for returning wounded soldiers and sailors. At the Newport Naval Hospital, women served as officers in the Navy Nurse Corps, and other women served as technicians, nursing assistants and in other posts.

Naomi Craig, a black woman who had operated an elevator at the Outlet Company prior to the war, in 1988 summarized how work opportunities in private industry expanded for women during the war:

WAVES recently arrived at Quonset Point, inside a Quonset hut, July 24, 1945. *Naval History and Heritage Command.*

When the war came, women went to work for the first time in factories and driving trucks. If a delivery truck came to your house, a woman would be driving it. The women were postmen. Up until that time, we didn't have women postmen. The women were garbage people. They were because all the available young men were in the service.

I started work in a war plant, Federal Products in Providence, where they made gauges and precision instruments. They taught us how to make these micrometers....I did it so well that I could take tension in my fingers to know just how a gauge would run....People came in from the government telling us that we were part of the war, that we had to do the best we could....We had such a feeling of being part of the war.

Women had always worked at Rhode Island's jewelry factories and textile mills. Many of the state's jewelry factories were converted into making medals and insignias for military uniforms. Women were deemed to be talented at this line of exacting work.

Brown & Sharpe, the state's largest private employer before the war, during the war "was pretty much run by women," Louise Aukerman recalled. She worked at one of its plants that made parts for ammunition.

Virginia Miller was nineteen when she was hired at the Naval Torpedo Station in Newport. "It was the patriotic thing to do," she said. Two of her brothers were in the service, one in the army air corps, the other in the marines. Born Virginia Calabani and raised in Newport's North End neighborhood, she worked in a tool crib keeping track of machine tools used to make torpedoes. And the pay was great. Miller earned about forty-seven dollars a week, big money at a time when the average pay for women in manufacturing jobs was about thirty dollars a week.

In 1942, Shirley Halsband spotted an advertisement in the *Providence Journal* inviting women to take an aptitude test. Soon she was part of a workforce that assembled the famous Oerlikon-Gazda 20-millimeter antiaircraft guns, which were installed on most U.S. Navy ships during the war. "One of the things I had to learn was to take apart and reassemble a gun," she said to the *Journal* in 1999. "It was quite a challenge. It was difficult, but I did it."

A few men resented the women, especially older men who were too old to serve in the military but had endured long apprenticeships learning their trades. "The engineers refused to deal with us. Those men thought women should be home, washing the dishes and the floors," Halsband commented. She tested precision instruments in various machine shops in the Blackstone Valley for the Oerlikons.

Women making bayonets, probably at the Imperial Knife factory in Providence. *War Department short film on Rhode Island wartime industry, courtesy of BuyOut Footage.*

At the Providence Shipyard, women not only proved they could be welders, they also ran lathes and drill presses and could be found in every other department as well. The use of women sometimes created tensions, because of the union pay scale. Once any welder passed a certain threshold, under the union contract, the hourly wage increases were automatic, increasing over time and reaching the then-astounding amount of $1.28 per hour. This reportedly created an issue with some male welders, who initially were more experienced and doing more work than their female counterparts but were not paid for the extra labor.

However, most of the dozen or so women interviewed by the *Providence Journal* in 1999, including Virginia Miller, said that most men at the Providence Shipyard treated them well and did not discriminate against them. Rather, the war bred a camaraderie among workers. "The men I had contact with were like fathers to me. They were very helpful," said Adelaide McLaughlin of Cumberland, who worked for both Brown & Sharpe and Walsh-Kaiser. Some of the men teased the women. "They'd say things like the ships are going to sink with all these women working on them. Of course they never did," said Claire Shippee, a Walsh-Kaiser welder.

Mildred Chatalian of Richmond, a housemaid before the war, learned to run a drill press and helped make rifle parts. She recalled her wartime work experience:

Job situations were a dime a dozen at this time because all the men had gone, and they were trying to get as many women as they could to replace the men in some of these jobs that required quite a bit of knowledge about machines. They were setting up trade schools where women were taught to read blueprints, charts, how to read a micrometer and how to operate a lathe and a drill press. They had you make a small screwdriver from scratch: the blade, the shaft, and the handle, and then put it all together. You learned the operations of the machine by making the screwdriver. I learned more or less how to operate some of the machines. One of the jobs I had was at Brown & Sharpe where I worked a lathe and I had to turn down bar stock into a certain diameter....I worked there about a year or so. Then I worked at Habledoff in Providence where I made wire assemblies for what they called depth tanks. Then I worked on Liberty ships down at Fields Point. I got 91 cents an hour. I went from 82 cents to 91 cents an hour, and that was in 1944....

On one job I wore bib overalls, and in the machine shops you had to wear what you call denim for aprons because it absorbed the oils and greases and you could wipe your hands on it and be sure it wouldn't go through to soil your clothing. You also had these wipe rags which were a heavy cotton material. You could wear your own shoes, but you wore the oldest ones because the floors were mostly oily, and you didn't want that getting on your good shoes.

Women with children often worked late shifts to tend to family during the day. Rose Amore of Pawtucket recalled starting her welding work at midnight at the Walsh-Kaiser Shipyard after taking care of her two children all day. Her husband served in the army. "I didn't sleep much in those days," said Amore. After she went to work, a neighborhood friend looked in on the children.

In 1942, the federal government for the first time required equal pay for men and women doing the same jobs in munitions factories and in army and navy facilities. But companies sometimes skirted these new laws, and enforcement was spotty. Brown & Sharpe in Providence was cited in 1942 by the government for paying women 20 percent less than men, according to a 1999 *Providence Journal* article. In 1944, the year before the end of the war, women in U.S. manufacturing had average earnings of $31.21 per week, compared to $54.65 for men.

Still, women made great strides. The median income for all women, adjusted for inflation, rose 38 percent during the war. Before the war, Selma Gallo, as with other women in the low-paying textile or jewelry shops, earned fifty cents an hour or less. Gallo fondly remembered her years repairing airplane wings at the Naval Air Station at Quonset.

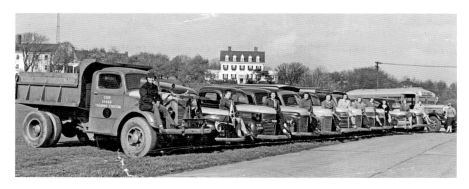

These women served the navy in Newport during the war as truck, bus and car drivers, jobs traditionally held by men. *Naval War College Museum Collections*.

Katherine O'Grady quit her job as a waitress earning fifteen dollars per week to work at a local woolen mill that had a defense contract to make blankets for soldiers. Her pay increased to twenty-seven dollars per week, which she used to support her child while her husband served with the Seabees in the Pacific. The factory earned an "E" for excellence in work, allowing the mill to place an E on the flag that flew over the plant. "We were very proud of it, because it meant that we were doing our part," O'Grady remembered.

Before the United States' involvement in the war, black women faced more discrimination in obtaining well-paying jobs than white women. Of 1,100 black women employed in Rhode Island in 1940, 831 were in domestic service. "We couldn't get a job in a store downtown. At the counter of the five-and-ten, they wouldn't hire us," recalled Eleanor Keys, who grew up on Friendship Street in Newport.

Wanting to employ all of the country's labor resources to win the war, President Franklin Roosevelt told the nation in one of his fireside radio chats, "In some communities employers dislike to hire women. In others they are reluctant to hire Negroes. We can no longer afford to indulge such prejudice." In 1941, Roosevelt issued an edict to prevent discrimination in hiring. As a result, income for black families doubled between 1939 and 1945. While at least one Rhode Island factory refused to hire black women during World War I, claiming that white women did not want to work with them, that kind of segregation did not occur in the state during World War II. Eleanor Keys was hired and trained at the Torpedo Station as a draftswoman, a skilled trade making engineering drawings.

Grace Straiten, a black woman who worked as a welder for Walsh-Kaiser from 1941 until the war's end, recalled how she found out about the job opening at the Providence Shipyard. "A friend told me, 'Girl, they're making big money down at the shipyard. Let's go get us some of that good money.'" Starting out at $0.85 per hour, Straiten was eventually paid $1.28 an hour working as a welder, rising up to a first-class position. Straiten said she vividly recalled feeling the winter winds that whipped into the shipyard off Narragansett Bay. "I had on long johns, slacks, and welding pants, and I was still cold. But I liked working there. I met so many people; we were like a big family." Straiten's sister and other family members helped out by caring for her two children while she welded Liberty ships.

Some women were not thrilled with the increasing role of women employed in traditionally male jobs. Referring to women who were hired to run the screw machines at Brown & Sharpe in 1942, Helen Clarke Grimes of Providence complained that such women were "very cocky" about it and would "swagger about the streets, dirty, coarse, swinging dinner pails as if they had waited for this all their lives." Later, she further lamented, "Women by the thousands have become greedy for money," many of whom "boast that they never made so much money in their lives."

Grimes then found it necessary to get a job in 1943, and she worked as a clerk at Brown & Sharpe in the Hospital Trust Building. She enjoyed the work and her colleagues, but she noticed a liberalization of sexual mores during wartime. While most of her female colleagues were a "moral bunch," some of the others "make you afraid to share the same restroom....Myra sins so steadily it is no longer news. She tells of all her exploits....So much getting in and out of bed with alacrity numbs one's interest." Grimes also complained of couples making out in movie theaters and of not being able to walk down Westminster Street "without inviting unwelcome attentions."

The newly wedded Ruth Barclay Stokes of Newport and Archie William Stokes in September 1941. During the war, Ruth and her sister Delores worked at the Naval Torpedo Station on Goat Island, while Archie served in the army in North Africa and Italy. Three of Ruth's brothers from Newport also served in the army. One of them, Alfred Steward Barclay, a pilot in the famed Tuskegee Air Corps, was killed in a training accident in 1944 at nineteen. *Keith Stokes Collection.*

Some women also contributed to the war effort by entertaining homesick soldiers and diverting them from dwelling on what lay ahead of them in Europe and the Pacific. Local women would organize USO and other events, and young women would attend them. For example, Marjorie Chase Sheldon summered at a house in Saunderstown on Narragansett Bay. She organized events at the nearby Dunes Club for officers stationed at Quonset Point, who were permitted to use the club's facilities. Officers at nearby Fort Kearney would sometimes stop in for dinner at her house, and afterward, with her two college-age daughters, they would all join in singing songs as one of the officers played the piano. A Coast Guard patrol boat's station was near the house. Marjorie's youngest daughter, Louise, recalled, "We became friendly and we had them over for swims and a meal many times." Marjorie would leave a towel on a fence to indicate to them when a cake had been baked. Louise and her older sister, Elisabeth, would often socialize with navy pilots at the Dunes Club. "Several of the fighter pilots we knew thought it was daring to fly under the Jamestown Bridge and a couple did," recalled Louise. "Flying under the bridge was forbidden to them as extremely dangerous!" Louise also recalled the excitement the pilots expressed when a new type of plane arrived for them at Quonset, especially the F6F Hellcat.

Elisabeth loved to hear the PBMs (Martin PBM Mariner flying boats) and PBYs (PBY Catalina flying boats) roaring over her house at 7:30 in the morning, on their way to antisubmarine patrols in Block Island Sound, Long Island Sound and the Atlantic Ocean. She and Louise would each sail a fifteen-foot wooden sailboat up the bay to Quonset Point to meet the seaplanes when they returned and landed on the bay at about 3:30 p.m. "The cascade of the water spray when the PBMs landed was beautiful," Elisabeth fondly remembered. After landing, the plane's crew would crowd around the exit door, gawking at the sisters in their bathing suits sailing their boats. Louise also recalled, "My sister and I loved to sail around the moored PBYs and talk to the crews. It was a long haul back to Saunderstown against the prevailing breeze." Tragically, two Quonset-trained pilots with whom the sisters had become close were killed a few days before the end of the war when their PBM collided with another PBM flying at night over Formosa.

Another eighteen-year-old, Eileen Hughes of Narragansett, volunteered to spot planes, logging some 1,500 hours during the war. "As a young person, I went to a lot of USO dances on Saturday nights. That was volunteer and kind of fun. All of these men that were stationed around here were young boys, all away from home who couldn't always get home for the holidays. So we'd invite them home for Sunday dinner and things like that," recalled Hughes. Eventually, she worked at the Naval Air Station at Quonset Point, making more money than her schoolteacher mother.

In 1943, local women near Davisville formed a CB-ettes Club at the Advance Base Depot at Davisville. They helped young Seabees away from home with routine chores, such as with letter writing and setting up long-distance phone calls to family members. In Bristol, Rebecca Chase Herreshoff organized a women's auxiliary motor corps to transport patients to area hospitals.

As the war wound to a close in 1945, women left the defense factories. Some were pushed out of the good jobs to make way for the returning veterans. "The women were the first to go," recalled Eleanor Keys, who left the Torpedo Station (but later earned a total of thirty years' service working at the Naval Underwater Ordnance Station). Many women left defense plants voluntarily, some as soon as their men returned. "I missed the friends I had made. I missed the money. But I was glad it was over. My husband came home," said Rose Amore. Having done their part, women were ready to settle into family life. The baby boom was about to occur.

Although many young women left the workforce to begin families, overall, married women's employment outside the home continued to rise after the war and has been rising ever since. The genie was out of the bottle and could not be put back in.

The Rise of Day Nurseries
in Providence

By Maureen A. Taylor

As men rushed to enlist for the war, they left jobs behind—creating a void in the workplace. Employers encouraged women to apply, but many female employees came with a complication: young children. Initially, government publications suggested that businesses hire only women without children or those with children over the age of fourteen, an unrealistic proposal. There were women with young children who sought employment and required childcare during work hours.

Free federally funded childcare centers administered by the Works Progress Administration (WPA) existed for individuals on relief. The WPA day nurseries began as a social welfare measure to enable lower-income families to seek employment. Parents who could afford to pay the fees had to find private childcare and babysitters. It was middle-class working mothers who faced a childcare crisis.

In 1942, addressing the need for more help for middle-class working mothers, the WPA expanded nursery services to include children of defense workers. Newspaper articles in Providence's *Evening Bulletin* proclaimed that preschool, which was once available only to the rich and poor, was now available to all.

The WPA operated two types of day nurseries, A and B. The first was free, while the second charged a fee. Neighborhood need determined their locations. A group of interested women could approach local WPA officials about opening a nursery in an area. In 1942, the WPA program ceased operation, but the Federal Works Agency agreed to administer the nursery program under pressure from women and employers.

Starting in August 1942, partial funding came from the Community Facilities Act, with 50 percent of the funding coming from communities. This act funded public works projects such as childcare centers in areas affected by the defense industry. Since many of its factories retooled equipment to provide materiel for the war effort, the City of Providence was eligible for funding but was also required to pay its share of the costs. The Providence City Council addressed the operation of the childcare facilities by appropriating $1,000 on September 26, 1942, for the establishment of a type B nursery school because of the large number of married women entering the defense industry. The program was referred to as the Nursery School Project.

In "Day Nurseries Saved in State," the October 1, 1943 *Providence Journal* reported that Rhode Island governor J. Howard McGrath felt that the demand for these centers would increase due to the draft and the number of women being employed in the war industry. He directed the state director of education to divert funds to keep the centers open.

At the huge Walsh-Kaiser Shipyard in Providence, which employed more than three thousand women, there were no daycare facilities, even though industrialist Henry J. Kaiser had established them at other shipyards. His Rhode Island workers used public childcare centers.

"The work at home is actually harder. You see at the Yard the shifts are of eight hours duration. At home, it's twelve hours with no relief," remarked Lena Pomoransky, a shipyard welder and mother of three, in the October 20, 1943 issue of the *Yardarm*, the weekly newspaper of the Walsh-Kaiser Shipyard. The *Yardarm* showcased women as capable workers but also reported on the various beauty contests held regularly on the third shift.

The *Yardarm* promoted the use of nearby nursery facilities, one for children from age two to school age and a before-and-after school program for children of school age. The cost per child ranged from $1.75 per week if the mother was the sole supporter of the family to $3.00 per week for a six-day work week. Discounts were available to parents with more than one child enrolled. This was a good rate, considering that female welders could earn the then-astounding pay of $1.28 per hour. According to the September 22, 1943 issue of the *Yardarm*, the women's counselor at Walsh-Kaiser Shipyard handled all enrollments for its employees at various private and government daycare centers in the city.

Promotional news articles in the *Providence Journal* and the *Evening Bulletin* fought the stigma attached to prewar childcare centers as being for the poor.

The original caption read, "Woonsocket, Rhode Island. This young lady's mother works in a war plant. The youngster passes twelve hours a day from Monday through Saturday in one of the 35 War Nurseries conducted for war workers' children." *FDR Library*.

They stressed the educational and social advantages for children in the programs, reassuring mothers that they could concentrate on their jobs while at work. "It is a world of small compass in miniature for little people who have the gift of being happy," wrote George C. Hull in the February 7, 1943 edition of the *Providence Journal*. He reassured parents that day nurseries were a safe place for their children while they worked.

A daily regimen included outdoor time, learning opportunities and personal hygiene such as teeth brushing after meals and hand washing, thus stressing the positive factors for families leaving their children in their care. They would be given breakfast and lunch every day with the added incentive of extra dessert for those who finished their meals. At the start of every day, children were examined for signs of illness and, if found to have a cold or a fever, were sent home.

The Family Security Committee of the Providence Civilian Defense Council, in conjunction with the Rhode Island Department of Education, operated the day nurseries at public schools. The October 1, 1943 *Providence Journal* reported that Providence had four centers in neighborhoods with high concentrations of factory workers. Centers operated at the Thurbers Avenue School, the Chalkstone Avenue School, the Veazie Street School and the Windmill Street School. In February 1943, a total of sixty-five children were enrolled. Due to demand, the hours they were open expanded from 7:30 a.m. to 5:30 p.m. to 6:30 a.m. to 6:30 p.m.

To encourage enrollment in after-school programs, the press also focused on the problems of "latch-key" children. There were dramatic statements of five- and seven-year-olds being allowed to care for themselves until their parents arrived home from work. Those parents were encouraged instead to use the after-school programs, which were designed to accommodate elementary school children. The Family Security Committee also hoped to care for teens.

Privately funded day nurseries were available too. The Salvation Army, the Carter Day Nursery administered by the White Sisters and the Providence Day Nursery of Nickerson Settlement House all operated daycare centers for children of working parents. The daily routine in their day nurseries was the same, except that the surroundings were different. Instead of being located in public schools, these organizations had their own facilities.

In 1944, the Providence Day Nursery cared for eighty-seven children from sixty-five families. At the end of the next year, it still had seventy-seven children from sixty-two families. With its nursery filled to capacity, parents waited months for an opening. Nickerson House operated a daycare center for children from six to twelve years old; these children also received medical and dental care.

At the conclusion of the war, many women lost their jobs to returning servicemen. The public childcare centers closed because of a perceived decline in need, but the private facilities continued to offer their services. Many women continued to work, still needing daycare for their children. The 1945 Annual Report for the Providence Day Nursery stressed that the need for childcare "grew even after the return of the veteran fathers, for wages were lowered and mothers continued to work."

The U.S. Army Handles Coastal Defense

By Brian L. Wallin

During World War II, the U.S. Navy located some of its most important U.S. operations in Narragansett Bay, including the Torpedo Station and Training Station at Newport, the PT boat training center at Melville, the Naval Air Station at Quonset Point, the Advance Base Depot and the Naval Construction Training Center at Davisville and the Advance Base Proving Ground at Allen Harbor. In fact, the navy operated a total of ninety-three functions in the state, down to a small recruiting center in Providence. Moreover, there were numerous key defense factories and shipyards in the state, including the massive Walsh-Kaiser Shipyard at Field's Point in Providence. It was the job of the U.S. Army to provide coastal defenses to protect these vital war efforts.

In early 1942, shortly after America's entry into the war, Rhode Island was declared a "military district" and then a "vital war zone," superseding the authority of the civil government. Blackouts, strictly enforced, were imposed as far north as Woonsocket to reduce the danger to coastal shipping from marauding German U-boats. Large parts of the coastline and bay were declared off limits, or access was restricted. Close attention was paid to factories producing military goods and military bases to prevent sabotage and espionage. Volunteer civilian aircraft spotters also played their roles. Beach patrols were conducted by the Coast Guard and civilian volunteers. More than four hundred marines helped to guard naval facilities. But a larger and more formal system of U.S. Army defensive fortifications was needed to protect Narragansett Bay.

Even before war was declared, the federalized 243rd Coast Artillery Regiment of the Rhode Island National Guard was already on duty at coastal forts on the bay. It was joined by other federalized guard units, including the 207th and 10th Coast Artillery, 211th Field Artillery Battalion (whose 105-millimeter howitzers were placed in areas not well covered by the fixed coast artillery), 181st Infantry Regiment (which augmented coastline patrols), 22nd Quartermaster Regiment (a segregated black unit) and the 132nd Engineer Battalion. By 1943, more than three thousand soldiers were assigned to the Harbor Defenses of Narragansett Bay.

Coastal defense was not glamorous, but the stateside duty was deemed vital for the war effort. All of the forts and other coastal defenses constituting the Harbor Defenses of Narragansett Bay were under the command of headquarters at Fort Adams, which in turn reported to Eastern Defense Command in Boston. The two army commanders who operated out of Fort Adams for most of the war were Brigadier General Arthur G. Campbell, followed by Colonel C.P. Pierce.

With the United States' entry into World War II looming, Fort Adams at Brenton Point in Newport; Forts Wetherill and Getty on Jamestown; and Fort

Battery No. 211 at Fort Greene at Point Judith in Narragansett under construction, February 17, 1942. *U.S. Engineer's Office.*

Kearney at Saunderstown in Narragansett served as the backbone of the coastal defenses. Fort Adams, commissioned on July 4, 1799, was the oldest coastal defense fort and the only one with classic stone walls. The remaining forts were established from the late 1800s to the early 1900s. Except for Fort Adams, they were deactivated after World War I but reactivated before Pearl Harbor. Efforts were made to update their weaponry, representing some two dozen types of different caliber heavy weapons. The guns included 10-inch disappearing rifles, which were raised up on their mountings to be fired and then dropped back down for reloading. Early twentieth-century 12-inch mortars at Forts Adams and Greble quickly proved outdated and were removed. (The Civil War–era Fort Greble, on Dutch Island, was not reactivated.) The other installations, called Endicott forts, maintained combinations of 12-inch, 10-inch and 6-inch artillery pieces, all aimed toward Rhode Island Sound, waiting for possible attack by enemy forces.

A two-gun artillery battery utilizing massive 16-inch naval cannons was installed at each side of the entrances of Narragansett Bay at two newly established forts: on the east side in 1941, at Fort Church in Little Compton on Sakonnet Point; and the other on the west side in 1943, at Fort Greene in Narragansett at Point Judith. Capable of firing a 2,250-pound projectile more than twenty-five miles out to sea, the guns were placed in casemates under cover of twenty to twenty-five feet of reinforced concrete that were connected to underground supply facilities by a network of tunnels. The 400,000-pound guns were originally intended to be used on battleships, but this use was canceled as a result of the limits under the 1922 Washington Naval Treaty. In the meantime, they were stored at the Watertown Arsenal in Watertown, Massachusetts. In early 1941, they were transported to Rhode Island by the New York, New Haven and Hartford Railroad on specially designed flatcars. They were then offloaded by railroad steam cranes onto heavy-duty trailer trucks and slowly driven down local roads to their destinations at Fort Church and Fort Greene, respectively. Additional 6-inch guns in shielded barbettes were also added at the water's edge.

Sixteen cleverly disguised concrete-reinforced fire control points, for directing fire from coastal artillery—mainly from Fort Greene and Fort Church—were established along the coastline from Watch Hill into nearby southeastern Massachusetts, as well as on Block Island. Some of these were also equipped with searchlights and radar. All were primarily manned by the 243rd Coast Artillery Regiment.

As attention gradually focused on threats from enemy submarines and small boats, heavy weaponry was replaced by 155-millimeter, 90-millimeter and

A massive 16-inch gun is being transported past the Stone Bridge Inn in Tiverton to its destination at Fort Church in Little Compton in early 1941. *Fort Adams Trust.*

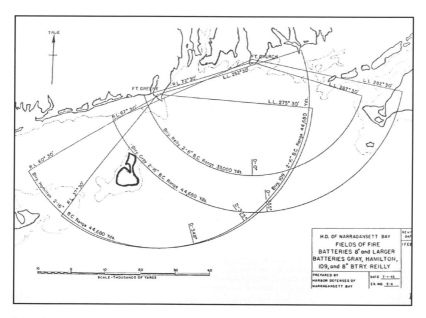

Map showing the range of the 16-inch cannons at Battery Hamilton at Fort Greene in Narragansett and at Battery Gray at Fort Church in Little Compton, as well as the 8-inch cannon at Battery Reilly at Fort Church. The 16-inch cannon at Fort Greene covers Block Island, while the 16-inch gun at Fort Church covers western portions of the Elizabeth Islands and Martha's Vineyard. Original map prepared in February 1943 and revised in February 1945. *U.S. Army, Harbor Defenses of Narragansett Bay.*

40-millimeter batteries at various sites along the coast, such as at the battery of mobile 155-millimeter guns on flat, circular cement Panama mounts opposite the Oaks Inn in Westerly and along Ocean Drive in Newport.

While no shots were ever fired at an enemy target during the war, army records show that all of the weaponry was fired in practice. The huge 16-inch guns at Forts Greene and Church were test fired in 1943, at a cost of $3,000 per shot. Neighbors complained when their houses shook and windows shattered.

Another new coastal defense installation, completed in 1941, was Fort Varnum, named in honor of Brigadier General James Mitchell Varnum of the Continental army during the Revolutionary War who hailed from East Greenwich. Located on thirty-three acres on the waterfront in Narragansett, the fort housed a pair of 6-inch rapid-fire guns relocated from Fort Getty and a battery of 3-inch guns moved from Fort Kearney. Later, four 90-millimeter anti-boat batteries were added.

Additional defenses came from the navy's Anti-Aircraft Training Center on Price's Neck in Newport. Several antiaircraft and anti-boat batteries were also located in and around Newport. A unit of the 207th Coast Artillery Regiment provided antiaircraft protection for the torpedo factory on Goat Island.

Beavertail, at the tip of Conanicut Island, was blocked off to civilian access by the army in 1942 and renamed Fort Burnside, in honor of Civil War general Ambrose Burnside, later a Rhode Island governor and U.S. senator. It became the location of the Harbor Entrance Command Post, a radio transmitter and radar facilities that supported harbor and coastal defense. Fort Burnside was also equipped with a powerful searchlight battery and underwater sound-detection devices. A pair of 3-inch guns relocated from Fort Getty and a new 6-inch artillery battery provided site defense. In

An aerial image of Beavertail Point on Jamestown in 1946, showing the Coast Guard Station at the southern tip; the Harbor Entrance Command Post in the middle on a rise of land; and radar antennae behind it on the left. *Jamestown Historical Society*.

the fashion of other fire-control points along the coast, reinforced concrete fire-control posts at Beavertail, Fort Varnum and Fort Greene were disguised as farm silos or summer cottages with wooden shingles.

On Block Island, the military observers manning the observation and fire control stations lived in the cottage-style quarters that had been built to disguise the sites from seaborne enemies. Like those on the mainland, the observation posts were equipped with sensitive range-finding equipment that was linked to the area's Harbor Defense Command Post at Beavertail. A radar station, disguised as a water tower, was added at the Southeast Lighthouse site on Mohegan Bluffs late in the war.

A major component of Narragansett Bay defenses were the antisubmarine and anti-boat nets stretched across both the East Bay and West Bay entrances, with electronic minefields added. The West Passage was protected by an immovable wire and net barrier strung between Fort Kearney in Saunderstown and Fort Getty at Jamestown. The East Passage, in the main channel, had a net barrier that could be opened and closed to allow ships in and out of the bay. It ran between Fort Wetherill to the west and Fort Adams to the east. There was also a second layer of nets in the East Passage. The nets were operated by the U.S. Army and supported by the navy's Net Depot and repair facilities at Melville. Due to the strong tides and wave action, the net minders confronted problems with holding the nets in place, and it took heavier and more numerous anchors to meet the challenge.

By 1944, the threat of seaborne or air attack had faded. The only possible threat was from German U-boats, and the antisubmarine nets already protected the bay. The four 16-inch guns at Forts Church and Greene, with their extended range, improved accuracy and increased armor-penetrating capacity, met harbor defense needs by themselves. No longer needed to host large-caliber artillery, Forts Kearney, Getty and Wetherill were essentially deactivated. At Fort Getty and other places along the Rhode Island coast, large-caliber coastal guns were replaced with anti-boat weaponry suitable to repel submarines or small surface attack craft, such as dual-purpose 90-millimeter artillery, 3-inch antiaircraft batteries and 37-millimeter anti-boat guns. The number of soldiers assigned to the Harbor Defense of Narragansett Bay shrank from about three thousand in 1943 to about five hundred by mid-1945.

In 1939, Hillsgrove State Airport in Warwick, still in its developmental stages as a civilian airfield, was chosen as the site of the National Guard's 152nd Observation Squadron. At first, the unit, with 12 officers and 183

A double layer of antisubmarine nets in the East (main) Passage extends from Fort Wetherill on Jamestown to north of Fort Adams on Brenton Point, May 28, 1942. Two small net gate vessels and one net tender monitor the nets, allowing boat traffic in and out, while two artillery pieces can be seen at Fort Wetherill. *National Archives.*

enlisted men, used World War I–vintage aircraft, and pilots paid for their own flying lessons. The troops lived locally and trained out of the airport's Hangar No. 1. They selected the famed Rhode Island Red Rooster for their shoulder patch. (On December 27, 1938, the airport had been officially renamed in honor of U.S. senator Theodore F. Green of Rhode Island, but it took some time for the new name to stick).

With the outbreak of war, the army absorbed the National Guard unit, took control of the airfield—calling it Hillsgrove Army Air Field—and added hangar facilities. As it was the state's only commercial airfield, limited public service was allowed to continue on a portion of the base. Hillsgrove operated as an auxiliary facility to Connecticut's Bradley Field outside Hartford. After the 152nd was later transferred to Fort Devens, located in Ayer and Shirley, Massachusetts, beginning in the summer of 1942, the army used Hillsgrove for training its 325th Fighter Group, which

A 6-inch gun at Battery 211 at Fort Greene at Point Judith, about 1944. *Christopher Zeeman Collection.*

flew P-40 Warhawks and later P-47 Thunderbolts. In 1943, the 325th moved to North Africa and then to Italy, where it saw heavy action.

With the training of new pilots at Hillsgrove came tragic accidents. On October 13, 1942, the 325th suffered its first fatality, when a pilot lost control of his P-40 and crashed at Norwood, Massachusetts. On February 11, 1943, four U.S. Army Thunderbolts took off from Hillsgrove in foggy conditions, on a routine flight to the army's Trumbull Field at Groton, Connecticut. Two crashed; a third is still officially missing; and a fourth has never been found. The pilots, all inexperienced and only one of whom had been certified to fly by instrument, hailed from the 352nd Fighter Group, then based at Trumbull Field in Groton. It was later determined that the operations officer on duty that day at Hillsgrove was not familiar with local weather patterns and should not have permitted the pilots to fly in fog, given their lack of experience in flying using instruments, which was necessary to do in fog.

Not all accidents were fatal. For example, on September 1, 1944, a Thunderbolt crashed in the bay near Warwick. The pilot, unhurt, was rescued by two young boys in a rowboat.

Hillsgrove was turned back over to the State of Rhode Island in September 1945. The Air National Guard returned and stayed until it moved to its own facility at Quonset Point in 1980.

While top-secret installations abounded in Rhode Island, one of the most unique was a highly secret, heavily guarded radio listening post located on Chopmist Hill in northern Scituate. The seventh-highest point in the state, Chopmist Hill was determined to be an ideal site to monitor enemy transmissions virtually worldwide around the clock. The largest of thirteen similar facilities in use around the country established by the Federal Communications Commission, its equipment was so sensitive that operators were able to listen in on communications between German tank units in North Africa and monitor Japanese transmissions in the Pacific. It was said that an intercepted transmission to German U-boats allowed the HMS *Queen Mary*, with more than ten thousand Allied troops on board, to evade enemy submarines.

High-powered radio receivers, located in an unobtrusive farmhouse, were served by a network of cleverly disguised antennae hidden by the tree line. Civilian linemen from Narragansett Electric Company were charged with changing the configuration of the antenna pole mounts to match new communication needs, never knowing their true function.

Chopmist was briefly considered as a possible site for the postwar headquarters of the United Nations, primarily because of its centralized communication potential. The site was passed over after the Rockefeller family donated land on Manhattan's east side for the organization.

The Top-Secret Prisoner-of-War Camp at Fort Kearney in Narragansett

By Christian McBurney and Brian L. Wallin

The site of the former Fort Kearney, at the end of South Ferry Road and about one mile south of the village of Saunderstown in Narragansett, is now occupied by the Narragansett Bay Campus of the University of Rhode Island. It may come as a surprise that in the waning months of World War II, this site served as the most unique prisoner-of-war camp for German captives in the country.

The story begins in the fall of 1944, when the Prisoner of War Special Projects Division was established by the Office of the Provost Marshal General. The Special Projects Division faced the daunting task of trying to "denazify" and reeducate some 380,000 German POWs housed in several hundred camps across the country. As an initial step, fanatical adherents to Nazism were identified and moved to a special maximum-security camp at Alva, Oklahoma. The goal was to prepare the rest of the German POWs to return to postwar Germany and serve as a vanguard promoting democratic ideals and a respect for peace. This would not be an easy task, as Germans had spent more than a decade under Hitler's iron-fisted rule, dominated by Nazi propaganda.

Lieutenant Colonel Edward Davison was appointed chief of the Special Projects Division. Davison, a former professor of poetry who would earn a Legion of Merit award for his wartime work, and his assistant, Major Maxwell McKnight, were hesitant to push for reeducation, fearing retaliation against American POWs held in Germany. In addition, the

Lieutenant Colonel Edward Davison, chief of the Special Projects Division. *Edward Davison Collection, Yale University Library.*

Geneva Convention prohibited the indoctrination of prisoners. However, it also encouraged "intellectual diversions" at POW camps. The Special Projects Division chose a small number of strong anti-Nazi prisoners to work at creating "intellectual diversions" for their fellow POWs, in what became known as the Idea Factory or just the Factory.

On October 31, 1944, the Factory began operating at a German POW camp in Van Etten, New York. But a larger site solely devoted to the Factory was desired. It was found at Fort Kearney, located on twenty acres in Saunderstown, Rhode Island, overlooking the West Passage of Narragansett Bay and Jamestown.

Named in honor of Philip Kearny, a Union general killed in the Civil War, some time prior to World War II the U.S. Army added an extra "e" and began spelling the name of the fort as Kearney. (Some elderly Rhode Islanders who lived at the Narragansett Bay campus in the late 1940s and 1950s still pronounce Kearney as "Cahnee" rather than the correct "Keernee.")

At the start of World War II, this so-called Endicott fort was armed with heavy artillery designed to reach far out to sea. As the threat of enemy attack had diminished by the start of 1945, Fort Kearney's artillery was removed and the fort was deactivated. With barracks for prisoners and their guards, as well as a kitchen and administrative buildings already in place, Special Projects Division inspectors liked what they saw, and on February 27, 1945, Fort Kearney was reclassified.

The first approximately eighty-five prisoners chosen for the special duty at Fort Kearney were a group of former German professors, writers and artists who had successfully passed a number of evaluations confirming that they were ardent anti-Nazis. Most had served in the German army against their will, some had spent time in Nazi concentration camps and all of them wanted to work to make Germany a different and better place after the war. Their story at Fort Kearney is not only how they helped to reeducate the German POWs at other U.S. camps but also how they rose to become influential postwar writers and thinkers.

Kearney's commander, U.S. Army captain Robert L. Kunzig, was instructed to keep the camp's role secret for several reasons. For one, many Americans had lost loved ones in the war in Europe and understandably hated Germans. Furthermore, in early 1945, several newspaper columnists and radio announcers had already charged the War Department with "coddling" POWs. In actuality, many German POWs were not Nazi sympathizers and had fought for their country out of a sense of duty, pride or fear. In addition, secrecy was imposed out of a concern that the names of anti-Nazi "rats" and "traitors" could be smuggled back to Germany where their family members could suffer the consequences.

While some prisoners volunteered to work at Fort Kearney, others took unusual paths. Raymond Hörhager was a prisoner at a POW camp in Arizona when he made the mistake of making a casual derogatory remark about Nazis. Put on a mock trial at the camp by a Nazi officer, Hörhager was sentenced to be tried as a traitor on his return to Germany. The sentence for treason, of course, was death. Fortunately, the condemned man received help from a friendly camp guard who himself was a German Jewish refugee who had fled Germany in 1933. Two weeks later, Hörhager was taken to another camp, where he was vetted about his anti-Nazi views. Along with a handful of others, he wound up at Fort Kearney.

Franz Wischnewski, a twenty-four-year-old artist who had been captured in July 1944 as a junior officer in the 114th Division, recalled being summoned out of his POW camp at Ruston, Louisiana, and told to bring his belongings. Accompanied by American guards who acted as if they wanted to kill him, Wischnewski was taken on a three-day train trip, which likely ended at the Kingston, Rhode Island train depot, and then was brought to Fort Kearney. A grateful Wischnewski suggested

A military policeman stands guard at the entrance to Fort Kearney when used as a POW camp. *Edward Davison Collection, Yale University Library.*

that the writer Alfred Andersch be brought to Fort Kearney, and camp officials agreed.

Andersch had been a prisoner in the infamous concentration camp at Dachau. Forced to join the German army, in 1944, he deserted his unit in Italy on a bicycle and was captured by the Allies and brought to an anti-Nazi POW camp in Louisiana. Upset at being forced to leave this camp and go on a trip to an undisclosed location, on being dropped off at Fort Kearney one night in May 1945, Wischnewski later recalled, "tears welled in Andersch's eyes" when he realized that Wischnewski and other prisoners he knew "were waiting for him."

The Special Projects Division recognized that to gain the trust of these vetted prisoners and allow them to do their important work, it could not impose on them the same level of discipline as in other German POW camps. While Fort Kearney was surrounded by barbed wire, it had no armed guards in towers. Kunzig relaxed the discipline in his camp, explaining, "We had almost no problems at Kearney. Once in a while we'd have to sort of jack them up and make sure they kept their beds neat—try to keep it very military and correct." No prisoner ever escaped from Fort Kearney nor tried to do so. Andersch recalled that a loudspeaker on the roof of the mess hall "woke us up every morning with a Duke Ellington version of 'Lady Be Good.'"

In order to remain at Fort Kearney, POWs were required to sign a remarkable declaration, given that Germany and the United States were still at war. It stated, in part, "I declare that I owe no allegiance or loyalty to Adolph Hitler, the Hitler Regime, and the Nazi Party....I further declare that I will strictly refrain from any activity which might be detrimental or appear hostile to the United States Government or the American people. I believe in a democratic way of way of life and am opposed to any form of dictatorship."

Signing the declaration also meant the POWs had to renounce their German military ranks. This was intended to minimize potential friction and encourage an environment where all of the prisoners interacted as equals. But prisoners were required to wear clothes with "PW" imprinted on them.

The most important and time-consuming mission at Fort Kearney was the production of a German-language newspaper intended for distribution to all German POW camps in the United States. Called *Der Ruf*, or in English, *The Call*, the newspaper was, as proclaimed on its masthead, "edited and prepared by and for German prisoners of war." The primary goal of *Der Ruf* was to persuade German POWs to focus on the future rebuilding of their country and to abandon Nazi ideas. It was also intended to present the facts of the war honestly and to give an accurate picture of the American way of life. The paper was not intended to be a vehicle for voicing official American opinion or policy, although there were limits on what could be published.

The first editor-in-chief of the newspaper was Dr. Gustav R. Hocke, a prize-winning German novelist and newspaper correspondent who had been forced to serve as a civilian interpreter for the German army in Sicily before being captured in September 1944. Hocke was supported by a remarkable staff of writers and other intellectuals who not only wrote the articles but, led by Curt Vinz, also produced the layout of the newspapers at Fort Kearney. The newspapers were printed at a military facility on Governor's Island in New York City.

The first issue of *Der Ruf* appeared in 134 POW camp canteens on March 6, 1945. The War Department's role in promoting *Der Ruf* was not disclosed to POWs. The newspaper, with eleven thousand copies distributed and supported by five hundred advertising posters put up at the camps, created an immediate sensation. Nazis at a few camps bought the issues and burned them; at other camps, they threatened fellow prisoners who intended to purchase the newspaper. At Camp Helen, Texas, for example, Nazi prisoners described the first edition as "Jewish propaganda...not fit for

A copy of the upper fold of *Der Ruf,* November 15, 1945. *Christian McBurney collection.*

men." Yet prisoners at many other locations received the publication with "overwhelming enthusiasm" and responded by purchasing all of the copies at their camp canteens.

By the time the fifteenth edition was issued on October 15, 1945, after issuing editions twice a month, seventy-five thousand copies were being printed, and sales totaled more than seventy-three thousand copies. One copy could be read by numerous POWs, consistent with one POW's letter from Camp Concordia, Kansas: "We circulate [the paper] by exchanging and handing it over to others."

POWs became bolder in reading *Der Ruf.* "When I read this newspaper," one POW wrote in a letter to the editor, a Nazi "came up to my bunk and yelled, 'Traitors read such kind of newspapers,' and that if I continued reading it, he would try to kill me. I didn't pay much attention and continued to read the newspaper."

Captain Kunzig observed that the newspaper "was indoctrination by correct facts." German soldiers, he noted, "weren't used to correct facts and didn't believe what they saw in *Der Ruf* until time proved how right the [newspapers] were and how wrong [Nazi] communiqués were."

POWs wrote hundreds of letters thanking *Der Ruf*'s staff. Private Bruno Wittman from Camp Hood, Texas, complimented the newspaper profusely, adding, "What I like most in it is the truth, even if sometimes a bitter truth. But the eyes of many have now been opened." A few captives still had difficulty overcoming Nazi propaganda. Commenting on the statement in one edition that Hitler had declared war on the United States (which he had done a few days after the bombing of Pearl Harbor), one unbelieving POW wrote to the newspaper's staff, "I wonder whether you can't lie any better."

American supervisors of the production of *Der Ruf*, led by Walter Schönstedt, a German leftist émigré who had become a captain in the U.S. Army, encouraged free thought and gave the prisoners great leeway. Lieutenant Robert Pestalozzi, a Swiss American, worked closely with the German editorial staffers, earning both their esteem and affection. War Department and State Department officials reviewed drafts in English prior to publication but required few revisions. The "Kearney Spirit," mentioned by many of the Germans and Americans at Kearney, developed. The camp's German spokesman, Gerhard Weiss, defined it as "total cooperation between the Germans and Americans, without reservation."

The German writers did not always agree with their American military supervisors, but the Americans were remarkably tolerant and did not insist that writers publish articles in which they did not believe. The most significant dispute surrounded American insistence on the policy of "collective guilt," making all Germans responsible for starting the world war and for Nazi war crimes against Jews, Gypsies, Poles and others. But understandably, the Fort Kearney prisoners, some of whom had suffered in Hitler's concentration camps, entirely rejected this notion and refused to reflect that view in the newspaper. One time an American officer traveled from Washington, D.C., to object to a proposed story of a German poet's resistance to Hitler—the poet was ultimately shot dead by the Gestapo—on the ground that there had been no German resistance to the dictator. Irmfried Wilimzig, a ballet dancer before the war, argued with the American officer, recalling later, "They obviously had no idea how many people in Germany weren't Nazis." Wilimzig won the argument, and the piece was published unchanged. Still, there was room for compromise on both sides of this ongoing argument.

On May 8, 1945, Germany surrendered to the Allies. About a month later, the Office of the Provost Marshal, deciding that it was no longer necessary to keep its German reeducation program classified, issued a press release describing its work, including the production of *Der Ruf*. (The identity of Fort Kearney was still not disclosed.) In the press release, Brigadier General Blackshear M. Bryan, Assistant Provost Marshal, credited the newspaper, which had included accurate accounts of the progress of

Fort Kearney is to the left, Fort Getty to the right, the lighthouse on Dutch Island is to the north and Jamestown Bridge is in the distance. By German POW artist Walter Junge, *Der Ruf*, November 15, 1945. *Christian McBurney collection.*

the war in Europe, with the lack of "serious demonstrations in camps" when Germany's surrender was announced.

On June 28, the editorial staff presented a petition, signed by Hocke, Andersch and others, arguing, "After these ten issues it becomes evident that…*Der Ruf* cannot maintain its old standard of quality and liveliness behind barbed wire." The writers did not believe they could accurately describe American society without interacting with American civilians. Hocke, in particular, expressed frustration that he had "seen nothing of America except prisoner of war camps."

The main reason for their discontent was that they yearned for what POWs wanted most of all: to return home as soon as possible to discover the fates of their loved ones. Professor Howard Mumford Jones of Harvard University had led Fort Kearney POWs in operating a pilot school to reeducate selected German POWs—the forerunner of the schools later established at Forts Getty and Wetherill on Jamestown (see the next chapter). The first graduates had been brought to the front of the line for repatriation back to Germany. In return for their loyal work, the petitioners also wanted to be among the first to return to their homeland and not be left behind to train more POWs who would be bound for Europe ahead of them. The Special Projects Division was sympathetic and put them at the head of the line for return to Germany.

New editors, writers and production workers were transported to Fort Kearney and assumed their new positions in September 1945 and remained there until the paper was discontinued in late March 1946. One of the new writers was the intellectual Hans Werner Richter, captured with the 999th Division in November 1943.

The prisoners at Fort Kearney had several important missions besides publishing *Der Ruf*. One was to monitor the newspapers published at other POW camps—which were typically printed on mimeograph paper—to detect Nazi influence. The busy prisoners at the Factory also reviewed books proposed for use in POW classes, on library shelves and for sale in camp canteens and translated American classics into German. "They sold like hotcakes" in the POW camps, recalled one Kearney writer. After Fort Kearney prisoners translated pamphlets written by Professor Jones describing America's institutions, history and people (about 85 percent of POWs nationwide spoke only German), the pamphlets were distributed to POW camps.

Kearney prisoners also screened hundreds of radio programs and movies before they were shown at other POW camps and recommended to drop those that showed the dark side of American life (such as gangster films) or were deemed to be overly propagandistic. They even advised not to show films with bad acting and poor plots, to forestall Nazi POWs from arguing that American culture was shallow. While watching most films was optional (they were very popular), POWs were required to view films of German atrocities discovered at concentration camps.

On August 15, 1945, after hearing of the surrender of Japan, the American staff and the Fort Kearney prisoners celebrated the end of World War II. Following speeches from Captain Kunzig and Lieutenant Pestalozzi and a prayer by Captain Richard Chase, a Fort Adams–based chaplain, a group of German representatives congratulated the American officers on the Allied victory and solemnly promised "to cooperate, with all their strength, in the reconstruction of a new Germany in a peaceful Europe, based on the principles of democracy, humanity, and a sincere and enduring understanding of all mankind."

Life was not all work at Fort Kearney. In addition to viewing movies, prisoners were allowed on the rocky Narragansett Bay beach next to the camp. The prisoners had time to read, write, draw and paint. They spent much time discussing politics and culture not only among themselves but also with American officers at the camp.

German POW artist Franz Wischnewski, with production editor Curt Vinz (*sitting*). *Edward Davison Collection, Yale University Library.*

Life at the POW camp was "really quite beautiful," recalled Franz Wischnewski after the war. "Every day in Kearney was like Sunday." However, Gerhard Weiss noted one drawback of Kearney, the "small space on which we had to live during the last year," which meant that POWs could not play their favorite sport, soccer.

It appears there was little interaction between POWs and local residents before the war ended, but there was some after that. Alfred Andersch recalled in a 1978 letter to Walter K. Schroder, with evident bitterness, "there was no contact" between the POWs "and the civilian population, as it was strictly forbidden. I do not know a single instance where a German prisoner was granted permission to socialize with the Americans, be it inside or outside the camp. Those were the regulations."

On occasion, prisoners (presumably working in camp administration) would jump into army trucks and be driven over the bridge to Jamestown and then travel by ferry to Newport to pick up supplies for their camp. On the ferries, they would talk with the other passengers. "I know this was true at Kearney," explained Kunzig, "because I sent them." Some stories go further and state that the other passengers did not know they were talking with German POWs, but that seems unlikely, given that the captives were always required to wear their prison clothes and typically had heavy German accents.

One Saunderstown resident, C. Michael Hazard, who was fourteen years old when the POW camp at Kearney opened, informed one of the authors, "It was no secret to those of us who lived in its vicinity. I don't remember seeing prisoners outside the camp, but I did get inside the facility on a regular basis, and the prisoners appeared to be a happy, well-fed group. We used to go down to the camp, pay ten cents and watch current movies with the prisoners."

Charles "Ted" Wright's family used to live at the corner of Boston Neck and Saunderstown Roads. He recalled that as a thirteen-year-old, he and his brother twice sneaked through the woods and walked up to the mesh fence surrounding Fort Kearney, where they engaged in pleasant banter with some POWs who were proficient in English. One POW even gave them a few cigarettes—apparently they were well provided for in that respect. Finally, an American officer, not wanting the POWs to mingle with locals, yelled at them in German, and the POWs left the fence.

It appears that after Alfred Andersch left for Germany, perhaps beginning in November 1945, a few POWs from Fort Kearney were allowed outside the barbed wire without escort. Ted Wright informed one of the authors that on a few occasions he saw POWs—in their prison clothes with "PW" stamped on them—walking north on Boston Neck Road (he suspects to the Twin Willows bar, which operated even back then). Neil Ross, who worked for eighteen years at the University of Rhode Island's Narragansett Bay Campus, over the years spoke with a few people familiar with the POW camp and heard that at the end of the workday and on weekends, the POWs were sometimes allowed to visit Wakefield, Narragansett and Newport unescorted, even though they were required to wear their "PW" garb. If these incidents did occur, presumably they occurred well after the end of the war.

While the German POWs thrived in the relaxed atmosphere at Fort Kearney, the same cannot be said of their guards. When Major Frank Brown—a stickler for discipline—visited the guard compound at the camp, he found that only one of the twelve guards stood at attention, with the remainder sitting or lying on their beds. Brown then had some of the guards transferred out of the post. By contrast, Lieutenant Colonels William Bingham and A.J. Lamoureaux of the First Service Command (covering New England), based in Massachusetts, were "proud" of Kearney, with the former calling it "the show place of the First Service Command."

The only known photograph of the *Der Ruf* editorial staff at Fort Kearney, probably August 1945. They are not wearing uniforms with "PW" on them. Alfred Andersch (*second from the left*) is wearing a sweater and smoking his pipe. *Edward Davison Collection, Yale University Library.*

By the time of the November 1, 1945 issue of *Der Ruf*, the attempts at German reeducation were publicized nationwide to fellow POWs. In an account of the reeducation program, a POW author wrote that the efforts at Forts Kearney, Getty and Wetherill were "probably unique in human history." The author explained, "Voluntarily, German prisoners of war have undertaken to start a work of positive aid to their own fellows here in captivity.…They did it as men who believe in the future of their home country, a country that must become a part of a peaceful world." The twenty-sixth and final issue of *Der Ruf* was distributed to camps on April 1, 1946.

The German POWs and their American supervisors at Fort Kearney performed important work disproportionate to their small numbers. They helped to reduce Nazi violence and influence in POW camps nationwide. They also helped to reduce tensions at the camps by accurately reporting war news. Most importantly, they helped to persuade many repatriated German soldiers returning to Europe to leave with a favorable impression of the United States and democracy. One survey of some twenty-two thousand prisoners concluded that 74 percent of German prisoners left with "an appreciation of the value of democracy and a friendly attitude toward their captors," while only 10 percent remained "militantly Nazi." These "reeducated" returning POWs would play a role in the remarkable postwar transformation of Germany. Even though Fort Kearney cannot claim all of the credit for this change in outlook, it deserves a healthy share.

Fort Kearney closed down in April 1946, and its POWs were eventually repatriated to Germany. By October, several of its buildings had been offered to Rhode Island State College (now the University of Rhode Island).

Alfred Andersch, Hans Werner Richter and Curt Vinz began to publish their own version of the *Der Ruf* newspaper in occupied Germany. Growing to a circulation of 100,000, it had a strong socialistic and democratic bent, and it also criticized American military occupation policy, sometimes harshly. Andersch and Richter wanted Germany to follow its own path and not be dominated by either the United States or the Soviet Union. With the Cold War between the United States and the Soviet Union heating up in 1947, American military authorities shut down the newspaper.

In response, Andersch, Richter, other POWs from Kearney and some of their friends formed what they called the Group of 47. The literary clique eventually included important writers such as Günter Grass and Nobel laureate Heinrich Böll.

In 1970, Alfred Andersch, who became a successful author in Germany, visited South Ferry after an absence of twenty-five years and once more looked out at the white lighthouse in mid-channel, at the low hills of Conanicut Island and at the mouth of the bay. In a 1978 letter to Rhode Island historian Walter K. Schroder, Andersch said, "The treatment we received in the American POW camps was excellent and a truly humane experience."

The Special Prisoner-of-War Camps at Forts Getty and Wetherill in Jamestown

By Christian McBurney and Brian L. Wallin

Among the several missions at the Idea Factory in Fort Kearney (see previous chapter), one was to establish an experimental school for a select number of anti-Nazi German POWs to undergo reeducation. Successful graduates were to serve as administrators, assisting U.S. military government personnel in postwar Germany. On March 19, 1945, the chief of staff of the U.S. Army approved the training of anti-Nazi POWs.

The talented commander of the Special Projects Division, Lieutenant Colonel Edward Davison, gathered a number of brilliant professors and other intellectuals to serve as teachers and lecturers. Of the eventual 101 POWs who would constitute the first class, the first 61 students arrived at Fort Kearney on April 28 and 29, 1945, even before the surrender of Germany the following month. The select POWs entered into a curriculum focused on English as a second language, military government and democracy. These classes were supplemented by informal discussion groups, visiting lecturers, quizzes and exams. The final stage included an interview to determine how much the POWs had learned and how useful they could be to postwar Germany and the American military occupation government to be established there. Once the POWs successfully completed the sixty-day program, they became eligible for early and direct repatriation to Germany. The program was found to be a success, with seventy-three POWs "graduating" at dignified ceremonies on June 29 and July 6 and then shipping off for Germany.

For the next phase of the reeducation effort, the War Department agreed to establish the U.S. Army School Center at two Jamestown locations: Fort Getty, which would house the Administration School for training future government administrators in postwar Germany (approved on May 19, 1945), and Fort Wetherill, which would house the Police School for training future policemen to work in occupied Germany (approved on June 2, 1945). The two camps were located on Conanicut Island, which encompasses the entire town of Jamestown. Fort Wetherill had a gorgeous position on the southeastern part of the island with a view overlooking the entrance to the East Passage of Narragansett Bay, while Fort Getty on the island's west side was directly opposite Fort Kearney across the bay's West Passage.

Lieutenant Colonel Alpheus W. Smith, a former English professor at Northwestern University and a World War I veteran, headed the two schools. As with Davidson, Smith would be awarded the Legion of Merit after the war. The total staff for the schools consisted of 58 officers, 115 enlisted men and 12 civilian consultants.

The Conanicut Island locations of Forts Getty and Wetherill were ideal places for POW facilities, since they were on a small island accessible at the time only by a bridge across the West Passage and by ferry on the island's east side to Newport. Early in the war, both forts had hosted coastal artillery units intended

An aerial view of Fort Wetherill, March 7, 1941. *Naval War College Museum Collections.*

to defend Rhode Island from seaborne attacks, but as that threat had subsided, the forts were largely deactivated. However, the wooden barracks, mess halls, administrative buildings and other buildings remained.

A rigorous selection process was undertaken to choose the POWs who would serve as the schools' students. German POWs wanted to enter the programs because they had learned that, despite Germany's surrender, they would be shipped to European countries to perform one or two years of forced labor. By graduating from Fort Getty or Fort Wetherill, the POWs could return to Germany and their families faster.

Candidates had to be anti-Nazi, trustworthy, loyal, industrious, age twenty-five or over and in good health; have a rank of captain or lower; and not display militaristic tendencies. Many, but not all, had graduated from college. The Special Projects Division whittled down a list of 17,883 POWs to just 816 suitable candidates for Fort Getty and 2,895 for Fort Wetherill.

A number of the candidates hailed from the 999th Light Afrika Division, most of which had surrendered before it engaged in any fighting. While many of these men were petty criminals, some had been political prisoners who had courageously resisted Nazism and been sent to concentration camps. Captain Robert L. Kunzig, the commander of Fort Kearney, recalled, "Everyone would say he was a professor or a political leader when he might be a murderer." But often it was fellow prisoners who exposed the fakers.

POWs arriving at Forts Getty and Wetherill underwent further vetting. On August 6, 1945, sixty-one POWs who had been sent to Fort Getty and then rejected, some for being Nazis, were transported by boat over to Fort Kearney. An American officer at the scene wrote a few days later that these POWs "were very downcast. We were all somewhat fearful that there might be some attempted escapes on the part of the prisoners" who had hoped to join the school as way to get back to Germany quickly. One of the Kearney POWs helped to defuse the situation.

The POWs who were selected to enter the schools at Forts Getty and Wetherill, as at Fort Kearney, agreed to renounce their military ranks so that all of the POWs could relate to each other as equals. They promised not to try to escape through the barbed wire. And they pledged that when they returned to Germany as civilians they would aid occupation forces governing the American zone in Germany.

POWs selected to be students were brought to Fort Getty secretly at night by truck. Wolf Dieter Zander, then a twenty-nine-year-old POW who had served as a junior officer in the 10th Panzer Division in North Africa, recalled the morning he was brought to Fort Getty. "The morning fog had prevented us from recognizing where we were, though we smelt the salt water of the sea. At noontime, after having several roll calls…the sun pierced through the fog and lifted the veil around us. We found ourselves on a small island, a rock in the sea.…We liked it from the first day, though [the sea] separated us from home."

The POWs were required to wear standard U.S. Army prisoner-of-war uniforms, with the large letters "PW" stamped on each item. But other than that, Fort Getty was an unusual POW camp. One of the instructors, James Ruchti recalled, "Instead of fences and guards…we had a three-strand barbed wire fence which we had to put up for token reasons." In addition, he remembered that some of the guards had been "a former prisoner of the Germans themselves…[and] therefore were very understanding of what it meant to be a prisoner."

Fort Getty's first classes began on July 19, 1945, with the sixty-day curriculum again focusing on the English language, German history, American history and military government. Fort Wetherill emphasized the last as part of its core mission to train policemen and thus spent less time on the other subjects. The primary idea that the instructors sought to convey to the prisoners was that democracy was not only a form of government but also a way of life that could serve as a guide for future behavior.

The enthusiastic spirit of Fort Kearney carried over to Fort Getty. Graduate Dr. Walter Hallstein later wrote, "The atmosphere in the stalag between the inmates, the teachers and the staff was terrific.…The selection of the faculty, and the methods they used to present the material made it very successful."

Wolf Zander recalled how he and his fellow classmates came to drop their suspicions and be open to learning: "The G.I. guard at the compound gate was…full of friendliness and willing to meet the other fellow half way. Then our instructors' missionary enthusiasm—an American trait which fascinates the tired, fatalistic European—would not fail to have its effect. Or it may have been our hosts' complete lack of prejudice. Or was it the landscape, the air, the rock in the sea?"

The most beloved professor was American history teacher T.V. Smith, a University of Chicago professor, author of bestselling books on American life, host of a popular radio show and a former congressman from Illinois. Then a lieutenant colonel in the U.S. Army, Smith emphasized the successful resolution of conflicts in American history, in contrast to the approach that had been followed in Germany of picking a leader who made everyone follow his policies. Yet he criticized the Civil War as a failure of U.S. democracy. The students were not accustomed to hearing such criticism. One POW recalled, "We were amazed at the frankness with which all the topics were

A U.S. Army sergeant teaches English to German POWs at Forty Getty, 1945. *War Department Film, Courtesy of Critical Past.*

discussed, as e.g., the Civil War was mentioned as a black point in American history." Smith later wrote that camp instructors were directed "to tell the truth" and "to be candid under questioning" by the POWs.

A favorite topic among the students at Forts Getty and Wetherill was the poor treatment of American blacks. T.V. Smith, a native Texan, found this topic easier to handle than his northern colleagues. He conceded his country's substantial shortcomings (a credit to him as a southerner in 1946) but asked his students to consider the progress blacks had made and requested suggestions from the students on how to improve their treatment.

Dr. Henry Ehrmann, a Jewish refugee who had fled Germany to escape Hitler, taught German history. Student Zander was deeply impressed that Ehrmann treated German POWs with the kindness and dignity that the professor had never been afforded in Germany. Another student remembered the school's emphasis that the prisoners had to learn to think for themselves and not passively accept dogma.

Fort Wetherill also used a staff of police officers and commanders from New York City, Cincinnati and several other cities as teachers of police methods. Major Kenneth K. Kolster, the Police School's commander, stated that the school emphasized decentralized police control of Germany on a local basis, in contrast to the centralized control of the Gestapo.

American instructors learned German traditions as well. "At the end of my first lecture," said a lieutenant, "the class began to stamp on the floor like a herd of buffalo. I was so scared I almost called the MPs. Then I found that stamping on the floor is the German student's way of applauding." Students would show their displeasure by scraping their feet back and forth on the floor.

The screening for the first class at Fort Wetherill was poorly done. A total of 258 POWs arrived at the camp by tarp-covered trucks at 1:30 a.m. on August 10, 1945, for the initial class. Due to transfers from Fort Getty, this total was increased to 294. But as a result of further screening, including the taking of polygraph tests by policemen from around the country, 139 were rejected before the first class even began. These men failed to meet the stated criteria, with explanations such as "strong Nazi leanings," "Hitler Youth" and "probably Gestapo." Communists were also rejected. Eventually, 145 POWs from the initial class graduated on October 13, 1945.

At any one time, there were typically about 200 students at Fort Getty and 150 at Fort Wetherill taking classes. Other POWs were usually at the camps, getting screened and waiting to start their classes.

There was not much interaction between the POWs at Forts Getty and Wetherill and Jamestown residents, but there was some. POWs were not allowed to stroll around town unescorted. However, they could use the beach near the school, and a few Jamestown residents remember seeing some of them on work details. As set forth in the August 5, 2010 edition of the *Jamestown Press*, Alcina (Lopes) Blair, a lifelong resident of Jamestown, recalled that as a young teenager, she saw "prisoners go by in trucks." She surmised that they were on their way to the garbage dump as they traveled along Southwest Avenue. Another longtime Jamestown resident, Delores Christman, when she was fifteen years old, remembered the POW trucks going up and down Southwest Avenue to and from Fort Getty. "They would wave at us, and we would wave at them," she said.

One night, Blair further recalled, two prisoners—who had gotten lost—appeared on the front porch of her family's house on Windsor Street. "My mother and father were concerned and called the chief of police who came and got them," she said. "They were not escaping. They were lost."

At the two camps, only one POW from Fort Getty escaped. He was Gerhard Hetzfuss, aged thirty-two, a former private in the 999th Division. The FBI, state police and police in various southern New England communities joined in trying to capture him. It was disclosed that the prisoner had been due to be returned to Germany in a few days prior to his escape in late January 1946, and he had run off with his American girlfriend. The two were captured in a hotel room in New York City. Rather than return to a devastated Germany, Hetzfuss wanted to start a new life in America. It is not known if his female friend worked at Fort Getty or helped him to escape, or both.

A Getty graduate, Heinz Härtle, corresponded for many years after the war with Chaplain J. Edward Elliot, who had befriended the POW at Fort Devens in Massachusetts. One letter, dated April 25, 1946, reveals the time it took for a POW arriving at Getty to begin and finish classes, return to Germany and get a job.

Härtle had been forcibly drafted into the German army in late 1942. In North Africa, he deserted to the Allies, winding up as a POW at Fort Devens. After undergoing a rigorous screening process there and volunteering for the school at Fort Getty, Härtle was taken by a "comfortable bus" past Providence and then to Jamestown, probably around July 25, 1945. After arriving at Getty, Härtle had a few weeks at "the wonderfully situated camp" to enjoy "swimming and fishing." In early August, he underwent further interviews and other screening. Finally, he was accepted into the school and started classes on September 3. After the "hard" but exhilarating courses, Härtle graduated and received his Certificate of Achievement on October 20. Just nine days later, he embarked from Boston on a ship bound for Germany.

After landing in Europe, he crossed into Germany on November 9 and was discharged as a POW on November 16. It then took him ten weeks to receive permission to travel through the Russian zone, which he needed to do to reach his small apartment in bombed-out Berlin. Still wondering if his wife had survived the war, he finally received a letter from her—she was alive, and the apartment was somehow unscathed. After an excruciating wait, he finally received approval to travel to Berlin and probably reached it and reunited with his wife in early February 1946. He had not seen her in three years, two months and three days. Fortunately for the Härtles, they lived in the American sector in Berlin, where Heinz Härtle obtained a job with American occupation forces as a court interpreter.

On May 28, 1945, after Germany's surrender, the Office of the Provost Marshall General declassified the reeducation program for POWs and announced it to the press. This was likely in response to criticism from some congressmen and members of the press for the government's failure to take advantage of the opportunity to rehabilitate German POWs, while the Soviet Union was suspected of indoctrinating its POWs about the benefits of communism. It was not until August 23, 1945, that Rhode Islanders for the first

Lieutenant Colonel T.V. Smith speaks at a POW graduation ceremony at Forty Getty, 1945. *Edward Davison Collection, Yale University Library.*

time were officially informed of the reeducation roles of the POW camps at Forts Getty and Wetherill.

From May to October 1945, five sixty-day training cycles were conducted, which produced a total of 1,166 German graduates. Each graduation ceremony was held at the Fort Getty theater, with Lieutenant Colonel Alpheus W. Smith addressing the graduates. One POW graduate typically gave an address as well, including Wolf Zander, who remarked, "What sincere and deep faith in man must live in a people [Americans] who conceived a school like this and made it a reality." After this address and ones by Lieutenant Colonels Davison and Smith, the POWs stamped their feet rhythmically for several minutes.

Pleased with the success at Fort Getty, the Office of the Provost Marshall General decided to expand the program to handle substantially larger numbers of POWs by creating another school at Fort Eustis in Virginia. Starting on January 6, 1946, some twenty-two thousand POWs attended the rapid six-day program at Fort Eustis before being returned to Germany.

While the courses at Forts Getty and Wetherill made a deep impression on a personal level on many of the POWs, the hope that they would serve as a vanguard to spread American ideals throughout

German society was overly optimistic. Their numbers were simply too small—1,166 men in a country of 65 million people. America had the best of intentions but lacked the time to reeducate many POWs before their return to Germany.

Many of the graduates had difficulty coping in postwar Germany. It did not help that some sixty thousand Germans, many elderly, died of starvation or exposure in the winter of 1946–47. Thirty-nine-year-old Konrad Sperber, in June 1946, informed a newspaper reporter, "It's sad but true that some of us don't feel safe to go around flashing the diploma we received from the course in democracy at Fort Getty." The former POW concluded that while U.S.-style democracy was workable in Germany, it would be a long haul at best.

In a 1948 survey of seventy-eight Getty graduates, most of the men complained that "Nazi and militarist elements are met everywhere," and nearly half of them claimed that "widespread corruption, red tape, and the low level of both morals and morale in all aspects of public and family life" formed their first and most shocking impressions of their homeland. Almost half of them were thinking about how they could leave Germany, with the United States the preferred destination. Many of them did immigrate to the United States, including Wolf Zander, who became a successful businessman in New York City.

Still, many graduates became leaders in postwar Germany. In 1958, Dr. Walter Hallstein, the most prominent of the Getty graduates, was elected the first president of the European Economic Community and served in that important capacity for ten years. His right-hand man in the EEC, Heinz Henze, was another Getty graduate.

Of course, Germany eventually did develop a successful democracy. Perhaps the most effective argument for democracy among most German POWs was the visible affluence of America and the kindness of its people. The latter point was expressed in a letter written by former German POW Willy O. Jaeger in 1991 to a Lawrence, Kansas newspaper. "With this letter I want to express my thanks to all the Americans who were kind to us, who didn't treat us as enemies or Nazi criminals but as humans. In the long run this was a much better way to make us friends of the Americans, working better than any reeducation."

By the fall of 1946, many of the buildings at Forts Getty and Wetherill had been abandoned. What had been Fort Getty is now a Town of Jamestown park, and Fort Wetherill is now a state park. Few park users know of the unique World War II history at the two former forts, including that the entrance gates still there at former Fort Getty were constructed by POWs.

The Battle of Point Judith and the Sinkings of *Black Point* and *U-853*

By Christian McBurney

Rhode Island's formidable defenses within Narragansett Bay were never tested during World War II, but the state has several notable claims when it comes to military incidents during the war. First, the last sinking of a U.S.-flagged merchant vessel by a German U-boat happened on May 5, 1945, less than three miles southeast of Point Judith. It was also the ship sunk closest to the American mainland by a foreign power since the War of 1812. Twelve of the forty-six crewman of the coal-carrying ship *Black Point* were killed or drowned. In addition, a day later, the same U-boat that sank the collier was destroyed, again within sight of Point Judith. It was the last sinking of a German submarine by U.S. forces in World War II. It was apparently the only U-boat destroyed on the bottom of the ocean in U.S. waters. All fifty-five submariners aboard *U-853* were entombed in their submerged vessel at the bottom of Rhode Island Sound.

Concern about German U-boats arose early in the war, when what Germans called "wolf packs" of their submarines prowled the exposed and virtually unprotected East Coast, sinking hundreds of Allied ships. In 1942, nine merchant vessels were sunk by U-boats off the New England coast alone. U-boats were sinking Allied ships faster than the Allies could build them.

Newport was touched by the shock of a U-boat attack early in the war. Shortly after midnight on January 14, 1942, about sixty miles southeast of Block Island, *U-123* fired three torpedoes at close range at the Panamanian tanker *Norness*, carrying 12,200 tons of fuel oil bound for Liverpool, England. Most of the ship's Norwegian crew escaped in lifeboats after the first strike. After more than twelve hours, the destroyer USS *Ellyson*, on a training mission out of Newport, and a Coast Guard vessel rescued six officers and twenty-four crewmen, landing them at Newport at 9:30 p.m. A fisherman lifted eight crew members onto his boat and carried them to New Bedford, after which they were transported by navy automobiles to Newport. One crew member was killed in the attack, and one drowned when his lifeboat overturned, while another crewman was seriously injured and cared for at Newport Naval Hospital. Rear Admiral Edward C. Kalbfus, the senior officer commanding navy operations in Narragansett Bay, reported the sinking to the commanding admiral of the Eastern Sea Frontier command in New York City, the details of which were shared with the press.

The navy's Rhode Island operations had as a mission searching for and destroying U-boats. Destroyers operated out of Newport, and a few PT boats came from Melville, while submarine spotting and killing aircraft flew from Quonset Point. Few U-boats ventured close to Narragansett Bay. German navy captains could sink just as many Allied ships somewhere else, farther away from a major navy base (at Newport) and the largest navy air station in the Northeast (at Quonset Point).

Tiny Block Island, sitting out in the ocean thirteen miles off Rhode Island's southern coast, played a unique role. The U.S. Navy authorized a reconnaissance patrol made up of fishing boats from the island (as well as Point Judith) to report on the sightings of periscopes and surfacing U-boats. German submarines would occasionally surface to recharge their batteries—sometimes among a fleet of fishing boats. "We called in three subs," recalled Silas "Dub" Barrows, one of the Point Judith fishermen who was given a radio by the navy. In addition, eight tall concrete lookout towers were erected on Block Island to watch for enemy submarines, ships and planes. Lookout towers were also erected on the coasts at Sachuest Point in Middletown, as well as in Little Compton, Narragansett and other locations.

Finally, by the late spring of 1943, increasingly effective submarine hunting by destroyer escorts; escort carriers carrying Wildcat fighters and Avenger torpedo and dive bombers; and land-based "flying boats," with the invaluable assistance of more effective radar, turned the tide in what was called the Battle of the Atlantic. Suddenly, U-boat hunters became the hunted. The heavy toll on German submarines was typified by the sinking of *U-550* by destroyers off Nantucket Island on April 16, 1944. One of *U-550*'s survivors, Günther Heder, was brought to Newport Naval

Hospital but died three weeks later of his injuries. He is buried under a headstone bearing his name at Newport's Island Cemetery Annex.

By 1944, the threat of attack from enemy ships and submarines was deemed to be so slight that several of Narragansett Bay's coastal forts had been deactivated. In early May 1945, within days of the end of the war in Europe, that situation changed. *U-853* entered Rhode Island Sound.

U-853, commissioned on June 25, 1943, had a reputation for escaping from perilous attacks. The submarine, 252 feet long and with a beam of 22 feet and 8 inches, had conducted two previous war patrols, sinking two ships amounting to 5,783 tons. On its second war patrol in May 1944, after sighting and chasing the massive HMS *Queen Mary*, which had been converted into a troop carrier, *U-853* was attacked while riding on the surface by three British Swordfish aircraft but escaped unharmed. Then, on June 15, 1944, U.S. Navy escort aircraft carrier USS *Croatan* (which would visit Quonset in February 1945) and several destroyers caught *U-853* on the surface, but the submarine dived and escaped again. Two days later, two aircraft intercepted *U-853*, killing two submariners and wounding the commander and eleven others, but the submarine was able to submerge before it could be destroyed.

On February 23, 1945, after being repaired and refitted, *U-853* and its fifty-five-man crew began its third war patrol, joining four other U-boats in an effort to attack U.S. coastal shipping, with the hope of improving Germany's bargaining position should Hitler seek a conditional surrender. *U-853*'s new commander, Captain Helmut Frömsdorf, was just twenty-

German submarine *U-853* is commissioned on June 25, 1943. *Naval War College Museum Collections.*

three years old, but he had been second in command on the submarine's second patrol.

After departing its base from Stavanger, Norway, *U-853*'s Atlantic crossing was slow, as Frömsdorf kept his submarine submerged as much as possible to avoid being spotted by Allied aircraft. On April 23, 1945, *U-853* torpedoed USS *Eagle Boat 56*, a World War I–era patrol boat off Portland, Maine. A total of fifty-four sailors met their deaths, and only thirteen survived, making it the worst loss of life during the war in New England waters.

After the U.S. Navy sent out ships to find the attacking submarine, the USS *Muskeogen* located by sonar what was probably *U-853* early in the morning of April 25 and attacked it, but no results of a hit were seen. A navy blimp was dispatched from the Naval Air Station at South Weymouth, Massachusetts, but its MAD detection gear malfunctioned.

The next day at 3:00 p.m., a radar operator in a plane whose squadron had taken off from Quonset Point and was flying over the Gulf of Maine detected a U-boat, which again probably was *U-853*. "The radar said there was a submarine sitting on top of the water about 40 miles away charging [its] batteries," recalled air crewman William Heckendorf. "We homed in on it and saw the oil slick on the water where it had been sitting. We dropped our sonar gear [called sonobuoys] and picked up the sound of a submarine's engine. We pinpointed the sub and dropped two 500-pound depth charges. About five minutes later the ocean was full of debris and oil." The submarine's skipper may have intentionally discharged oil and debris to fool the attackers into thinking that the submarine had been sunk. In any event, the U-boat's commander decided to change venues. If he was Captain Frömsdorf, he ordered his submarine to head for Rhode Island Sound.

On May 4, 1945, at 5:30 a.m. eastern time, Admiral Karl Dönitz ordered by radio all U-boats to cease hostilities. Captain Frömsdorf did not heed the message. He probably never received it. Most likely he stayed submerged as much as possible, during which time he could not receive messages from Germany. Or his radio equipment may have been damaged by the attacks on his submarine in the Gulf of Maine. Whether he never received the message or whether he received it and ignored it will never be known with certainty.

A strong indication that Frömsdorf did not hear the message was revealed in postwar correspondence between his sister, Helga Deisting, and his flotilla commander in Germany, Günther Kuhnke. According to Kuhnke, after *U-853*'s departure from Norway, he never heard from Frömsdorf again. Contrary to normal operating procedures, *U-853* failed to radio back to headquarters. Kuhnke thought that this approach kept the crew alive into May. The other four submarines all reported in regularly, but their messages were intercepted by U.S. intelligence forces, and each one had been sunk by early April. If the U-boat stayed underwater most of the time, it could have missed the radio order to cease military operations. According to Frömsdorf's sister, Frömsdorf was neither a fanatic nor a member of the Nazi party.

On the other hand, there is some evidence that Frömsdorf may have ignored the order to cease military operations. According to the widow of the first commander of *U-853*, Helmut Sommers, Frömsdorf was "very young and ambitious," and Sommers felt the need to "again and again" warn the young commander not to risk the lives of the crew needlessly. Frömsdorf's decision to steer *U-853* into Rhode Island Sound, so close to Newport and Quonset Point, could be considered evidence that the submarine commander had a desire to end his submarine's patrol in a burst of supposed glory. In addition, he chose to attack a freighter in water that was only about one hundred feet deep. Captain Sommers later told his wife that "he never had attacked a ship in such a situation" and that "*U-853* was lost from the beginning with such little water under the keel and so close to the coast." What actually motivated the young submarine commander will never be known.

In the late afternoon of May 5, Frömsdorf spotted in his periscope the SS *Black Point*, a 368-foot, 5,000-ton collier, built in 1918, carrying 7,500 tons of coal on a voyage from Newport News, Virginia, to Boston Edison's power plant at Weymouth, Massachusetts. Less than three miles southeast of Point Judith and about seven and one-half miles northeast of Sandy Point on Block Island, not seeing any enemy warships in his periscope in the East Passage to Narragansett Bay or elsewhere in Rhode Island Sound, the German captain ordered a torpedo to be fired.

In the minutes before the torpedo sped from the submarine, on board *Black Point*, radioman Raymond Tharl later recalled, "As far as anybody knew, the war was over." Believing his unescorted ship was in safe waters, its captain, Charles E. Prior, did not bother to post lookouts or zigzag to avoid submarine torpedoes. Most of the crew was eating dinner when Frömsdorf gave the order to fire.

At 5:40 p.m., *U-853*'s torpedo struck the vulnerable stern of *Black Point*. A staggering explosion rocked the collier, and chaos broke out on board. The stricken vessel's captain, in interviews with the *Providence Journal* in 1945 and 1985, said, "I don't mind telling you that it hit the fan all right. The mainmast went over the port side, and about everything on the bridge that was breakable did break. The vibration and concussion was really something. It blew open both doors of the pilothouse." He further recalled, "The stern of the ship was blown off and sank to the deck level immediately. The men below decks aft didn't have a chance."

Captain Prior gave the order to abandon ship and was the last survivor to leave his vessel. *Black Point* rolled over twenty-five minutes later and went down stern first, carrying the bodies of eleven crewmen and one armed guard with it. "It stood straight up and the last thing I saw was the belly of it," recalled merchant seaman Howard Locke, who saw it from a life raft crammed with sixteen other surviving crewmen. The stricken vessel settled on the ocean floor one hundred feet below.

One of the rescuing ships, the Yugoslav freighter SS *Kamen*, radioed a report of the torpedoing. At a command post at Point Judith, part of Fort Greene, Boatswain's Mate Joe Burbine, on watch at the time, had *Black Point* in view in his binoculars just as he heard a muffled explosion and watched it stagger to a halt. He also radioed in the incident and alerted gunners manning six-inch artillery pieces nearby. One of the messages was picked up by the First Naval District headquarters in Boston, which immediately alerted Eastern Sea Frontier headquarters in New York, which in turn started to assemble a search-and-destroy mission.

Receiving news of the sinking by radio, small boats streamed out of Point Judith, Quonset Point and Newport to rescue the surviving thirty-four crew members of *Black Point*. Rescue boats sent from Quonset Point picked up fifteen survivors, landing them at Newport. Coast Guard boats took in the remaining nineteen survivors from *Kamen* and a Norwegian vessel, landing them at the nearby Point Judith Coast Guard Station.

According to Professor Henry Keatts, at the time all of the destroyers operating out of Newport were on missions at sea, and none were nearby. Presumably, they, too, were hunting for U-boats, in light of all of the recent activity. Fortunately for the Americans, three antisubmarine warfare escorts from U.S. Navy Task Force 60.7 were already underway thirty miles to the southeast, steaming for Boston, after having just escorted an eighty-ship convoy from North Africa safely to New York City. They were the destroyer escorts USS *Atherton* and USS *Amick* and the Coast Guard patrol frigate USS *Moberly*.

Lieutenant Commander Leslie B. Tollaksen, commanding officer of *Moberly*, was the senior officer closest to Rhode Island Sound since Tollaksen's superior, Commander F.C. McCune, was on the destroyer escort USS *Ericsson*, by then far ahead in the western end of the Cape Cod Canal. Tollaksen ordered the three

The destroyer escort USS *Atherton* in search of *U-853* on May 5, 1945. *National Archives.*

warships to change course and steam at full speed toward the site of the *Black Point*'s sinking. Still, it would take them one and a half hours to arrive there.

Meanwhile, Frömsdorf decided not to surface his submarine and speed away from the scene, probably out of fear that he was near strong naval bases that could quickly react and begin searching for *U-853* by air and sea. But by staying submerged, the German skipper could only go at slow speeds as he headed out to the sea off Block Island.

Navy officers figured that *U-853* might seek shelter in the East Ground, a steeply rising shoal that could allow a submarine to lie alongside it and perhaps escape detection by sonar. There was also a shipwreck in the area, which it was thought the German U-boat captain might use to try to further confuse sonar operators. Tollaksen ordered a search across this area and back.

Arriving in the East Ground about 7:30 p.m., *Atherton*, *Moberly* and *Amick* formed a patrol line abreast and commenced their methodical search for the enemy submarine, using their sonar systems. In a surprisingly short time, the search plan worked. At 8:14 p.m., sonar men on *Atherton* located the submarine, about five miles east of Grove Point on Block Island. *Atherton*'s commander, Lieutenant Commander Lewis Iselin, ordered his destroyer to drop thirteen magnetic depth charges, each the size of a large trashcan, holding hundreds of pounds of high explosives that would explode on contacting a metallic object. One of them exploded with a powerful concussion, but it could not be determined if it hit the submarine or an old wreck on the ocean floor.

Iselin ordered a second attack with hedgehogs, which were projectiles that detonated only on contact and thus interfered less with sonar. But they could also explode on the hard sea floor. *Atherton* then lost contact with the U-boat, probably as a result of explosions interfering with its sonar. By this time, *Amick* had been ordered away to convoy a nearby merchant vessel, and Commander McCune had arrived on the destroyer *Ericsson*, assuming overall command.

Reinforcements arrived, including the destroyers *Barney*, *Breckinridge*, *Blakeley* and *Semmes*, the frigate *Newport*, the corvettes *Action* and *Restless* and some PT boats from Melville. McCune ordered them to maintain a barrier patrol around the search site, to guard against the U-boat slipping away to the open sea.

McCune ordered *Atherton* to search to the north and *Moberly* to the south. At 11:37 p.m., *Atherton*'s sonar relocated *U-853* lying still at a depth of about 109 feet and some 4,000 yards east of its previous position. The destroyer attacked with more hedgehogs, causing "[l]arge quantities of oil, life jackets, pieces of wood, and other debris, and air bubbles, coming to the surface." Knowing that shooting debris out of torpedo tubes was a ploy skippers often used to feign death, the assault continued.

After the attack was renewed, *Moberly*'s sonar man reported that *U-853* was moving again. Captain Frömsdorf was steering to the south at a speed of four to five knots. McCune ordered more strikes by both *Atherton* and *Moberly*, after which it was determined that the submarine was still moving, but at a reduced speed of two or three knots.

The damaged U-boat could have surfaced to fire its last torpedoes and go down fighting or even surrender. But Frömsdorf decided to stick with his original plan and continued to stay submerged. It was the captain's last mistake. Meanwhile, the crew must have suffered horribly as it awaited more attacks in the fetid air of the doomed submarine.

Both *Moberly* and *Atherton* dropped more depth charges. At about 12:44 a.m. on May 6, spotters on the *Moberly* saw bubbles, oil and a life jacket. Those on *Atherton* recovered a pillow, a life jacket and a small wooden flagstaff.

Kenneth Homberger, on board the *Atherton*, recalled many years afterward, "We always played tag out there with those subs, but we never really knew if we nailed one of them. This time we knew." He added, "We had a crackerjack sonar man. He would call out the bearings [of the sub], and the skipper would maneuver the ship." Homberger further recalled, "We finally sank that baby about midnight. I was manning one of the

Sailors on the Coast Guard frigate *Moberly* watch the surface boil as a result of a hedgehog attack on *U-853*. *National Archives.*

search lights. We saw a long line of bubbles coming up. Then there was oil and debris."

At 1:14 a.m., *Atherton* informed headquarters in Boston that the submarine was destroyed. Nevertheless, the complete destruction of *U-853* was not accepted by headquarters, and McCune continued his attack. The assault was pursued remorselessly through the night, with both depth charges and hedgehogs. The opportunity to work over a bottomed U-boat and practice firing live ammunition was a welcome one. *Atherton*'s commander Iselin recalled, "There was no doubt that by this time we knew we had it but it seemed everyone wanted to get into the act. I don't think there is a hull that took a bigger beating during the war."

After daybreak, a remarkable sight appeared on the horizon. Two navy blimps, *K-16* and *K-58*, from the Naval Air Station at Lakehurst, New Jersey, arrived and immediately located oil slicks and marked suspected locations with smoke and dye markers. Using MAD technology, their operators found a stationary target underwater—it probably was *U-853*. (Blimps would continue to be part of the U.S. Navy's antisubmarine force into the 1960s.)

At about 5:30 a.m., *Moberly* fired off more hedgehogs in the target areas. More debris rose to the surface, this time "German escape lungs and life jackets, several life rafts, abandon-ship kits, and an officer's cap which was later judged to belong to the submarine's skipper."

Finally, the blimps dropped sonar devices on the sea above the submarine. Sonar operators then reported hearing what they described as "a rhythmic hammering on a metal surface which was interrupted periodically." Perhaps it was made by a surviving German sailor hoping for rescue.

Moberly, and now *Ericsson*, as well as other ships whose commanders insisted on getting in on the action, continued the attacks on the helpless German submarine. The blimp *K-16* also fired 7.2-inch antisubmarine rocket bombs.

The firing ended at 12:07 p.m. on May 6, when Commander McCune at last convinced headquarters in Boston that *U-853* had been destroyed. Eastern Sea Frontier in New York City ordered the attacks to cease. It is likely the submarine was sunk sometime between midnight and 5:00 a.m. on May 6. Both *Atherton* and *Moberly* were given credit for the kill. *Atherton*'s captain Iselin later said, "I felt he [Frömsdorf] would be making for deeper water and I caught him before he got there." The American naval force had unleashed against *U-853* 264 hedgehogs and 195 depth charges, as well as 6 rocket bombs fired by the blimps. The German submarine had no survivors—its entire fifty-five-man crew was killed, probably from a combination of explosions, suffocation and drowning.

Later that day, a diver from the submarine rescue vessel USS *Penguin* found the wreck of *U-853* in 130 feet of water. He landed on the conning tower and reported that the submarine was lying on its side with its hull split open and bodies strewn about inside. He saw only two direct hits. That day and the next two days, navy divers attempted to enter the wreck to recover the captain's safe and the papers within but failed.

The Naval War College Museum at Newport has in its possession a letter, apparently written in about 1960, from the former skipper of the *Penguin* from May 29, 1944, to May 28, 1945, Lieutenant Commander George Waugh Albin Jr., to a chaplain at the Newport navy base that elaborates on the diving efforts made by him and his crew from May 5 to 7, 1945. Their mission was to rescue any surviving submariners (there were none) and to find the captain's log book (it was never found). Albin wrote

Two Coast Guard officers aboard *Moberly* show some of the articles that floated to the surface from *U-853*. *National Archives.*

of operations that occurred on May 7: "My diving officer, Chief Gunner Bockelman, and I made a joint dive in the vicinity of the conning tower and observed a hatch to be open. Mr. Bockelman, being quite small, wormed his way into the conning tower while I tended him and shortly thereafter pushed a body up to me which I moored a line to and had hauled up to the surface." The letter writer added, "As I recall, the name of this seaman was Hoffmann, a young lad of about 20, very well equipped in a black leather coat, his escape lung was on and ripped down the middle of the front as if it had suffered a sudden concussion after being inflated, possibly by a depth charge." A list of *U-853*'s crew includes Herbert Hoffmann, aged twenty-three at the time he perished off Point Judith. According to another diver, David Clary, Hoffman was later taken to *Penguin*'s home base, New London, where an autopsy was performed, which found that he had died from a concussion and that there was no water in his lungs. It is not known where the submariner was buried.

The former skipper of the *Penguin* wrote further, "Groping in the crowded conning tower, as I recall, Gunner Bockelman thought there were six other bodies and as we were about to take them out, orders came over the diving telephone relayed from Sub Base, New London, to secure all operations." The disappointed divers later learned that recovery operations were called off because the war against Germany was about to end (the war officially ended early in the morning of May 7) and because it was dangerous to dive around so much unexploded ordnance. (Gunner Edwin J.R. Bockelman was later awarded the Navy and Marine Corps Medal for his bravery in volunteering to enter the conning tower hatch.)

The sinking of *U-853* was immediately covered by local and national newspapers. On May 16, the Associated Press ran a photograph of Frömsdorf's hat and other items from the submarine recovered on the surface.

May 6, 1945, was far from the end of *U-853*'s saga. Recreational divers first visited the site in 1953. In the summer of 1960, Burton Mason of Trumbull, Connecticut, removed the remains of an unidentified crewman, which were buried with full military honors in Newport's Island Cemetery Annex on October 24, 1960. In attendance at that unusual ceremony were the German consul general in Boston, a commander of the German navy and naval officers from the Newport Naval Base.

Mason informed the press that he had found the skeletal remains of five members of the crew, still dressed in uniform, near the escape hatch at the conning tower. According to Mason, "Others were found near the escape hatches in both the forward and aft torpedo rooms. Each of them has an escape lung about his neck, which indicated that the crew was preparing to abandon the sub when they died."

Mason announced that he planned to raise the U-boat and have it publicly displayed in Newport. While Mason found surprising support from two of Frömsdorf's former superiors, Kuhnke and Sommers, Captain Robert Olsen, a successful submarine commander in the Pacific who had retired to Newport, opposed the effort, saying, "I shudder to think of the feelings of families of any of my former friends who lie off the coast of Japan." In January 1961, the Newport City Council and local clergymen

A display about the sinking of *U-853* on the grounds of the Naval War College includes the submarine's two propellers. *Brian Wallin.*

decried what they said would be the "desecration" of the remains of the submarine's dead crewmen. The State of Rhode Island also warned Mason, but the Connecticut man shrugged off the criticism; in fact, there was uncertainty at that time regarding how far the country's territorial waters extended.

On January 18, 1961, the West German government announced that *U-853* "is still owned by Germany and any action to surface the vessel or bring anything up from it is illegal." The Bonn statement also declared that "raising the sub would be akin to piracy." Undeterred, Mason blustered that he would move ahead with his plan to raise the U-boat. But he never did, probably because no one would provide financing for the expensive project.

In the years after 1960, divers clipped off the upper eight inches of the periscope as a souvenir. Various items were brought up by divers, including life jackets, boots, a steering wheel, gauges, a pistol and, distressingly, an occasional bone. In 1968, a private Delaware company failed to raise the submarine, reportedly stating that it had deteriorated to such an extent that it could not be raised.

Today, the site of the submarine is a popular, if dangerous, location for divers. Entering the wreck is risky because of debris, sharp metal edges and confined spaces. Three recreational divers have died from exploring the wreckage. The site of *U-853* is now considered a war grave, and it is illegal to remove items from it.

Recent divers have provided information that *U-853* sits upright currently, with its stern resting in 130 feet of water, while its periscope rises to a depth of 100 feet. The hull has two holes caused by depth charges or hedgehogs, one forward of the conning tower at the radio room and another in the starboard side of the engine room, and remains split open. Unexploded hedgehogs and depth charges surround the site. Rumors that the submarine carried a cache of gold proved false.

Tangible reminders of the Battle of Point Judith can be seen in Newport today. A white headstone in the Island Cemetery Annex marks the grave of an unidentified *U-853* submariner. The large bronze propellers that were raised from *U-853* are exhibited on the grounds of the Naval War College. Lewis Iselin, who would earn renown as a sculptor after the war, donated Frömsdorf's captain's hat and other debris from *U-853* to the Destroyer Escort Historical Museum in Albany, New York.

Navigation charts still flag *U-853*'s wreckage with this warning: "Danger. Unexploded Depth Charge. May, 1945." *Black Point*'s nearby grave is shown with two blue circles marking the bow and stern of the ship.

Reflection, Relief and Rowdiness

RHODE ISLANDERS REACT TO THE END OF WORLD WAR II

By Maureen A. Taylor

On May 8, 1945, at 9:00 a.m., civil defense sirens screamed across Rhode Island, followed by drivers honking their horns. The war in Europe was over! On the radio, President Harry S. Truman, who had assumed the office after the sudden death of President Roosevelt on April 12, announced the Allied victory in Europe. Nazi Germany was no more. Yet in the Pacific, the war continued its awful course. President Truman acknowledged that fact, exhorting, "We must work to finish the war. Our victory is only half over."

Governor Howard J. McGrath asked Rhode Islanders to "conduct themselves with reverent decorum befitting the magnitude and solemnity of the events which have brought us to this historic hour." He set an example by attending a noon Mass at the Cathedral of Saints Peter and Paul officiated by the Most Reverent Francis P. Keough, bishop of Providence. Bishop Keough added his own thoughts to the day's events, remarking that while there was reason for celebration, "there was no place for boisterousness or noisiness, because after all, this is not the end; it is only one phase of victory."

In Providence, thousands of people filled the streets. Fireworks day and night showed public enthusiasm for the victory. Newspaper editors compared the festivities to those that had surrounded the end of World War I.

Out of a fear that revelers would get drunk, Central Falls and Pawtucket locked saloons and restricted liquor sales. Still, Sergio Correira of Warren—with five sons in the military—raised a toast to the victory.

In Newport, the commander of all naval operations in Rhode Island, Commodore Clinton E. Braine, encouraged navy personnel to attend worship and to continue their jobs to help defeat the Japanese.

While Truman's message was intended to keep laborers on the job, across the state, with a few exceptions, defense workers left their stations, causing factories to declare a work holiday. At Gorham Manufacturing Company, however, workers continued their twenty-four-hour production of shells.

The initial enthusiasm of the occasion dissipated by afternoon. Folks went home for lunch, and a light rain fell. One town official compared it to a midweek Sabbath. Most stores and schools closed.

Cities and towns reported their communities quiet and pious, with many churches offering services. Pawtucket and Woonsocket residents briefly filled the streets and then went to church for prayer and reflection.

The official V-E Day of May 13, Mother's Day, lacked celebration. That day found people hoping for an end to the war on the other side of the world.

Three months later, on August 14, sirens screamed again—signaling the victory over Japan. Governor McGrath declared a holiday after Truman's 7:00 p.m. announcement. Throughout Rhode Island, banks, schools and public buildings closed. Other businesses shut down at their discretion. Police departments, alerted beforehand to the announcement, called in their day patrolmen. As a precaution, hotels in Providence ended liquor service following Truman's announcement.

V-J Day celebrations bore little in common with those of V-E Day. Four years of the stress of war was over, and everyone wanted to celebrate. Parishioners went to their churches to pray in thanks, but many found themselves part of noisy crowds in public places.

Forestdale native Nellie Moore Rollins, a member of WAVES, was in the barracks at Davisville. She summed up a common feeling. "We felt we'd been released. We were running out of the barracks." The women marched to areas of the base that had been off limits until that moment. "When we got over to where the flag was, I don't think you ever felt as patriotic as you did when that flag came down."

Flags and bunting appeared throughout the city of Cranston. Revelers filled the streets, many making their way to buses to take them to Providence. Children employed noisemakers of all sorts to mark the occasion. Horns honked throughout the night. Citizens of East Providence hung effigies of Hirohito from trees along major roads. In Pawtucket, a group of more than a dozen boys decided to march in an impromptu parade with flags, drums and noisemakers. Fifty years later, one of the boys, Phil Moran, recalled that it was "a day like no other." In Woonsocket, Jacqueline Gauthier, then fourteen, was at home on Paradis Avenue. "All the whistles were going, and the church bells," she recently recalled. "I wanted to go where all the action was, on Main Street. My mother said no."

The August 15 edition of the *Providence Journal* compared the festivities to a carnival. An estimated fifty thousand people filled downtown Providence, singing, dancing and shaking hands with strangers. Sailors and soldiers began kissing willing young women in jubilation. This was happening in other cities as well. A sailor and Rhode Island native, George Mendonsa of Newport, was in Times Square in New York City when photojournalist Alfred Eisenstaedt photographed him kissing a nurse.

As the party continued in Providence, it took a violent turn. Muggers began assaulting women, dragging them to the pavement for "sport." Vandals smashed windows in downtown stores and on trolley cars. Broken glass from liquor bottles littered the city streets. Young celebrants burned the playhouse on Garibaldi Playground and tried to do the same at Richardson Park. Bonfires burned on Federal Hill and in South Providence.

Police, firemen and shore patrolmen attempted to maintain order. Fire departments in all parts of Providence answered more than one hundred alarms, most of them false.

The official V-J celebration on September 2, during Labor Day weekend, was anticlimactic. Church services marked the occasion, but unlike on August 14, there were no crowds, no rowdiness and no extended celebration. Rhode Islanders were beginning to put the war behind them.

Thirty-five years later, in 1990, that Newport sailor who kissed a nurse in Times Square on V-J Day received a surprise phone call from a friend who told him that his picture was in a book published by *Life* magazine. George Mendonsa saw the picture for the first time at his home in Middletown. He was astonished and annoyed. He immediately recognized himself and began collecting details to prove his case. Mendonsa decided to sue the then owner of *Life* magazine for using his image without his permission.

Eisenstaedt was not the only photographer to capture an image of a U.S. sailor grabbing a nurse for an impromptu kiss in the midst of the Times Square V-J Day celebrations. Victor Jorgensen also photographed this couple. *National Archives.*

As the fame of the photo grew, more people wanted to know the names of the man and woman in it. Several men and women came forward claiming to be in the right spot at the right time. One man took a lie detector test to prove his claim. The photographer, Eisenstaedt, agreed with another of the claimants.

There are plenty of details in the picture worthy of analysis. The location is clear. The images were shot just south of Forty-Fifth Street looking north from a location where Broadway and Seventh Avenue converge. Location is a key part of every story told by men and women who later stated they were the couple. Not all of the stories lead those individuals to the right spot for the kiss. This was not the only couple who embraced.

The sailor in this shot shows his stripes on the right side of his uniform. Mendonsa clearly remembered placing them on that side on that day. Two of the other claimants were a lower rank than Mendonsa.

One of the details that make some television crime shows interesting is the study of facial features and other physical characteristics. There are at least twenty major points in a person's face worth comparing—eyes, ears, nose, mouth, hairline and the spacing of all those features. In this case, tattoos on the sailor's hand and the features of that hand also come into play.

Mendonsa's lawyer hired Richard Mead Atwater Benson, a nationally known photography expert. Details of the Benson report appear in *The Kissing Sailor: The Mystery Behind the Photo That Ended World War II*, by Rhode Islander Lawrence Verria and his coauthor George Galdorisi. Benson studied all the evidence, including details on Mendonsa's right arm and that of the sailor. A close look at a raised bump on the left arm of the sailor compared to one of the exact same size and location on Mendonsa's added further support for the identity. Benson concluded that Mendonsa was definitely the sailor in the picture. Fourteen years later, a team of experts compiled by the Naval War College in Newport used three-dimensional facial modeling to compare Mendonsa's face to the sailor's in the photo. They came to the same conclusion.

Life magazine continued to decline to name Mendonsa as the sailor. Mendonsa persisted in his efforts and found important support. Verria and Galdorisi, after compiling all the evidence in their book, called for an end to the controversy. Only Middletown's own George Mendonsa, they concluded, has the right stuff to be the man kissing a woman in the iconic photo celebrating victory.

The woman in the photograph, Greta Friedman, died in September 2016. She once said of Mendonsa, "The reason he grabbed somebody dressed like a nurse was that he felt so very grateful to the nurses who took care of the wounded."

Three years after the war, Rhode Island declared V-J Day a holiday. As other states stopped honoring the holiday, Rhode Island continued. In 1990, V-J Day became Victory Day. Today, Rhode Island is the only state to celebrate this holiday.

Location of U.S. Naval Aircraft in Rhode Island and Aircraft Types and Numbers—A Sampling at Various Dates

Naval Air Station Quonset Point

Seaplanes and Amphibious Reconnaissance Planes

Type	2/22 1942	4/22 1942	12/8 1942	5/31 1943	1/5 1944	5/16 1944	12/12 1944	4/15 1945	Totals
PBY-5A Catalinas	4	16	13	16	18	6	12	17	102
PBY-6A Catalinas	-	-	-	-	-	-	-	1	1
PBO-1 Hudsons	-	3	-	-	-	-	-	-	3
PB2Y-3 Coronados	-	-	-	-	3	-	-	-	3
PB4Y-1 Liberators	-	-	-	8	14	3	3	4	32
PBM-3 Mariners	-	-	-	3	5	15	12	8	43
PV-1 Venturas	-	-	-	25	36	6	6	2	75

Type	2/22 1942	4/22 1942	12/8 1942	5/31 1943	1/5 1944	5/16 194	12/12 1944	4/15 1944	Totals
PV-3 Venturas	-	1	-	9	-	-	-	-	10
SO3C Seamews	-	-	-	2	-	-	-	-	2
OS2N-1 Kingfishers	-	-	-	-	-	1	1	1	3
OS2U-3 Kingfishers	-	-	15	22	16	16	16	4	89
J4F-2 Goslings	-	-	-	-	1	2	1	1	5
J2F Ducks	-	-	-	3	-	-	5	-	8
Totals	*4*	*20*	*28*	*88*	*93*	*49*	*56*	*38*	*376*

Torpedo/Dive Bombers and Fighters

Type	2/22 1942	4/22 1942	12/8 1942	5/31 1943	1/5 1944	5/16 1944	12/12 1944	4/15 1945	Totals
TBD-1 Devastators	-	5	-	-	-	-	-	-	5
TBF-1 Avengers	-	-	9	33	65	35	24	9	175
TBM Avengers	-	-	-	-	13	47	80	61	201
SB2U Vindicators	-	30	6	-	-	-	-	-	36
SB2C Helldivers	-	-	-	-	36	37	49	10	132
SBD-4 Dauntless	-	-	9	-	-	4	1	-	14
SBD-5 Dauntless	-	-	-	-	48	27	12	5	92
F4F-4 Wildcats	-	-	-	4	12	-	-	-	16
F4U Corsairs	-	-	-	2	-	2	1	6	11
F6F-3 Hellcats	-	-	-	5	37	42	44	1	129

Type	2/22 1944	4/22 1944	12/8 1942	5/31 1943	1/5 1944	5/16 1944	12/12 1944	4/15 1944	Totals
F6F-5 Hellcats	-	-	-	-	-	-	55	23	78
FG-1 Corsairs	-	-	-	-	-	-	-	9	9
FM-1 Wildcats	-	-	-	-	18	1	-	-	19
FM-2 Wildcats	-	-	-	-	5	18	19	11	53
JM-1 Marauder	-	-	-	-	2	-	1	-	3
R4D-6 Transports	-	-	-	-	-	-	2	46	48
Other	-	-	-	-	6	6	6	8	26
Totals	-	*35*	*24*	*44*	*242*	*219*	*294*	*189*	*1,047*

Note: JM-1 Marauders were converted Martin B-26s.

Quonset Totals	**4**	**55**	**52**	**132**	**335**	**268**	**350**	**227**	**1,423**

NAVAL AUXILIARY CHARLESTOWN

Type	2/22 1942	4/22 1942	12/8 1942	5/31 1943	1/5 1944	5/16 1944	12/12 1944	4/15 1945	Totals
TBF-1 Avengers	-	-	-	-	9	1	-	-	10
F6F-3 Hellcats	-	-	-	-	39	91	54	14	198
F6F-5 Hellcats	-	-	-	-	-	-	101	117	218
SBD-3 Dauntless	-	-	-	-	-	3	-	-	3
R50-6 Transports	-	-	-	-	-	1	1	-	2
JRB-2/JRB-3	-	-	-	-	-	1	2	2	5
Totals	*0*	*0*	*0*	*0*	*48*	*97*	*158*	*133*	*436*

NAVAL AIR AUXILIARY FACILITY WESTERLY

Type	2/22 1942	4/22 1942	12/8 1942	5/31 1943	1/5 1944	5/16 1944	12/12 1944	4/15 1945	Totals
TBF-1 Avengers	-	-	-	-	14	-	-	-	14
F6F-3 Hellcats	-	-	-	-	-	12	40	8	60
F6F-5 Hellcats	-	-	-	-	-	-	-	19	19
SBD-5 Dauntless	-	-	-	-	-	1	1	2	4
Totals	*0*	*0*	*0*	*0*	*14*	*13*	*41*	*29*	*97*

NEWPORT NAVAL BASE

Amphibious Aircraft on a Cruiser (Launched by Catapult)

Type	2/22 1942	4/22 1942	12/8 1942	5/31 1943	1/5 1944	5/16 1944	12/12 1944	4/15 1945	Totals
OSU2-3 Kingfishers	-	-	-	-	-	-	2	-	2
SOC-3 Seagulls	-	-	-	-	-	-	-	1	1
SON-1 Seagulls	-	-	-	-	-	-	-	1	1
Totals	*0*	*0*	*0*	*0*	*0*	*0*	*2*	*2*	*4*

State Totals	4	55	52	132	397	378	551	391	**1,960**

Source: Location of U.S. Naval Aircraft Reports, 1942-45, U.S. Navy. Copies of originals available at Naval History and Heritage Command website: www.history.navy.mil (click on Research, Archives, Digitized Collections, Naval Aviation Records and finally Location of Naval Aircraft, WWII). Chart prepared by Christian McBurney, June 20, 2016. Training, U.S. Army and state National Guard aircraft not included.

Naval Facilities in Rhode Island in World War II Showing Peak Personnel at Each Location

Newport and Aquidneck Island

Activity	Officers	Enlisted	Civilians	Total
Naval Training Station	2,054	23,500	1,124	26,678
Naval Torpedo Station	285	1,440	12,900	14,625
Naval Hospital	96	533	196	825
Navy Nurse Corps	-	117	-	117
NOB Headquarters	95	496	1,742	2,333
Naval War College	362	41	53	456
Naval Net & Naval Fuel Depot	79	759	250	1,088
Anti-Aircraft Training Center, Price's Neck	302	1,500	-	1,802
Marine Barracks, NOB	15	489	-	504
Purchasing Office	11	-	84	95
Motor Torpedo Boat Squadrons Training Center	400	2,000	-	2,400
Motor Torpedo Boat Repair Training Unit	45	684	-	729
USS Constellation	4	130	-	134

Naval Air Station, Quonset Point

Activity	Officers	Enlisted	Civilians	Total
Naval Air Station	1,035	3,850	5,738	10,623
Advanced Aviation Training Unit	6	1,316	-	1,322
Fleet Air	865	5,850	-	6,715
Marines	19	406	-	425

Davisville

Activity	Officers	Enlisted	Civilians	Total
Naval Construction Training Center	1,059	23,028	111	24,198
Advance Base Depot	326	48,955	17,234	66,515
NOB Supply Depot	37	13	776	826
Narragansett Group	66	347	-	413

Totals	**7,278**	**115,337**	**40,208**	**162,823**

Source: Naval Operation Base—Newport, R.I. Administrative History, US Naval Training Station (Newport, RI) Records, Manuscript Collection 39, Box 10, Folder 8, Naval Historical Collection, U.S. Naval War College. Obtained by John W. Kennedy. Information not included: the Naval Hospital had 1,419 patients.

Bibliography

Chapter 1. Pearl Harbor Attack Panics Rhode Islanders

Books

Downie, Robert. *Block Island—The Land*. Block Island, RI: Book Nook Press, 2001.

Periodicals

Boston Globe, July 2, 1942, and October 27, 1943.

Cincinnati Enquirer, July 2, 1942.

Lancaster, Jane, ed. "'I Go into Detail Mostly on Account of Posterity': Extracts from the World War II Diary of Helen Clarke Grimes." *Rhode Island History* 63, no. 1 (Winter/Spring 2005): 3–24.

Morgan, Thomas J. "President Roosevelt Visits Newport." *Providence Journal*, August 12, 1990.

Newport Mercury. December 12, 1941, and July 3, 1942.

Providence Journal. December 8–10, 1941.

Original Sources

Sailing permit for Elisabeth K. Sheldon, June 6, 1944. Elisabeth Kellogg Sheldon Aschman Collection.

War Diary, December 7, 1941–December 31, 1942. Naval Training Station, U.S. Naval Station Files, Ms Coll. 39, Naval War College.

Chapter 2. The Torpedo Station at Newport

Books

Beach, Edward L. *Submarine!*. New York: Simon & Schuster, 1946.

Calvert, James F. *Silent Running: My Years on a World War II Attack Submarine*. New York: John Wiley & Sons, 1995.

Enright, Rosemary, and Sue Madden. *Historic Tales of Jamestown*. Charleston, SC: The History Press, 2016.

Gannon, Robert. *Hellions of the Deep: Development of American Torpedoes in World War II*. University Park: Pennsylvania University State Press, 1996.

A History of Torpedo System Development: Century of Progress, 1869–1969. Newport, RI: Naval Undersea Warfare Center, 1998.

Klein, Maury. *A Call to Arms, Mobilizing America for World War II*. New York: Bloomsbury Press, 2013.

Prichard, Walter. *History of the Naval Torpedo Station, Newport, RI, Chronological History 1869–1945*. N.p.: self-published, 1946.

Rowland, Buford, and William Boyd. *U.S. Navy Bureau of Ordnance in World War II.* Washington, D.C.: Department of the Navy, 1954.

Schratz, Paul R. *Submarine Commander.* Lexington: University Press of Kentucky, 1988.

Periodicals

Gould, Richard A. "Gould Island Naval Air Facility and Aerial Torpedo Bombing." *Rhode Island History* 52, no. 1 (February 1994): 21–29.

Jamestown Press. "Jamestown Historical Society Feature." March 28, 2013.

Nicolosi, Anthony S. "'Torpedo Range' Island: Gould Island, Narragansett Bay in the Second World War." *Newport History* 73, no. 251 (2004).

Oral Histories

Collart, Julien. Interview. July 3, 1985. U.S. Naval Torpedo Station 1937–1951. Newport Historical Society.

DiPretoro, Jack. Interview by Christian McBurney. June 14, 2016.

Stokes, Keith. E-mail message to Christian McBurney. June 3, 2016.

Stokes, Ruth Barclay. Interview by Keith Stokes. May 26, 2016.

Other

Irwin, Manley R. "A Note on Flawed Torpedoes: Congress as Shop Steward." Manuscript, Peter T. Paul College of Business and Economics, University of New Hampshire, Durham. N.d.

Shireman, Douglas A. "US Torpedo Troubles." *Military History* (blog). http://www.military.com/Content/MoreContent?file=PRtorpedo2.

"U.S. Naval Torpedo Station." Revised Report for USN Bureau of Ordnance Info No. 3–51. March 1951. Naval War College Archives.

CHAPTER 3. THE NAVAL AIR STATION AT QUONSET POINT AND THE NAVAL AUXILIARY AIR FIELDS AT CHARLESTOWN AND WESTERLY

Books

Building the Navy's Bases in World War II: History of the Bureau of Yards and Docks and the Civil Engineer Corps, 1940–1946. Vol. 1. Washington, D.C.: GPO, 1947.

Bush, George H.W. *All the Best, George Bush, My Life in Letters and Other Writings.* New York: Scribner, 1999.

Ignasher, Jim. *Rhode Island Disasters: Tales of Tragedy by Air, Sea and Rail.* Charleston, SC: The History Press, 2010.

Levine, Erwin L. *Theodore Francis Green, The Washington Years, 1937–1960.* Providence, RI: Brown University Press, 1971.

Morrison, Samuel E. *The Atlantic Battle Won, May 1943–May 1945.* Urbana: University of Illinois Press, 1956.

Mulligan, Sean Paul. *Quonset Point Naval Air Station.* 2 vols. Charleston, SC: Arcadia Publishing, 1996–98.

North Kingstown, Rhode Island, Statewide Historical Preservation Report W-NK-1. North Kingstown: Rhode Island Historical Preservation Commission, 1979.

Shettle, M.L. *United States Naval Air Stations of World War II.* Vol. 1. Bowersville, GA: Schaertel Publishing, 1995.

Periodicals

Carbone, Ged. "The Ghosts of Charlestown's Naval Auxiliary Air Station." *Rhode Island Monthly,* October 2011.

Cranston, Tim. "Hitler Trains at Davisville." *South County Independent,* September 13, 2001.

Providence Journal. "2 Planes Collide at Quonset Manor." April 23, 1944.

Quonset Scout. Several articles celebrating the second anniversary of Naval Air Station Quonset Point. July 14, 1943.

Standard (North Kingstown, RI). "Two Planes Crash at Quonset Manor." April 27, 1944.

Original Sources

Allen, William Slater. Speech on Charlestown Naval Airfield. Charlestown Airfield. Historical Subjects File. Naval War College Archives. Undated.

Crochet, Ernest. "Action of the USS *Ranger* (CV-4), From the Journal of a Signalman." www.airgroup4.com/crochet.htm.

Duggins, Marie Virginia Murdock. "A Connecticut WAVE at Quonset Point." June 24, 2016. http://smallstatebighistory.com/?s=Connecticut+WAVE.

"Fred Friendly's Speech at Quonset." *NPR.* Last modified October 1, 2005. http://www.npr.org/templates/story/story.php?storyId=3396086.

U.S. Naval Aircraft Reports, 1942–45. U.S. Navy, Naval History and Heritage Command. https://www.history.navy.mil/research/histories/naval-aviation-history/location-of-us-naval-aircraft-world-war-ii.html.

U.S. Navy booklet on U.S. Naval Station Quonset Point, circa 1944.

War Diary. First Naval District. March 1945. Record Group 38. National Archives.

Other

"Air ASW - World War II Years." http://www.globalsecurity.org/military/systems/aircraft/asw1.htmwww.fas.org (discussing MAD technology).

Augusta IV (CL-31). www.history.navy.mil (search for "Augusta" and "CL-31").

O'Connell, Charles, Jr. "Quonset Point Naval Air Station." Historic American Engineering Record. National Park Service. Department of the Interior. Washington, D.C., December 1979.

CHAPTER 4. SEABEES, PONTOONS AND QUONSET HUTS AT DAVISVILLE

Books

Building the Navy's Bases in World War II: History of the Bureau of Yards and Docks and the Civil Engineer Corps, 1940–1946. Vol. 1. Washington, D.C.: GPO, 1947.

Decker, Julie, and Chris Chiei, eds. *Quonset Hut: Metal Living for a Modern Age.* New York: Princeton Architectural Press, 2005.

Department of the Navy. *Naval Construction Battalion Center Davisville, Davisville, Rhode Island, A Historical Perspective, 1942–1994.* Washington, D.C.: Government Printing Office, 1994. Reprinted by Kenneth E. Bingham. CreateSpace Independent Publishing Platform, 2011.

North Kingstown, Rhode Island, Statewide Historical Preservation Report W-NK-1. North Kingstown: Rhode Island Historical Preservation Commission, 1979.

Schroder, Walter K., and Gloria A. Emma. *Davisville and the Seabees.* Charleston, SC: Arcadia Publishing, 1999.

Periodicals

McCarthy, Dave. "'Can Do' Veterans at Work on Seabee Memorial and Park." *Providence Journal*, December 15, 2004.

Reilly, George W. "Veterans' Journal. History of the Quonset Hut Lives On Today." *Providence Journal*, January 11, 2010.

Wallin, Brian. "The Quonset Hut: A Rhode Island Original That Went to War—Worldwide." *Varnum Armory Newsletter*, April 2016. http://varnumcontinentals.org/2016/04/the-quonset-hut-a-rhode-island-original.

———. "This Bee Really Stings: The Creation of the Seabee Logo." *Varnum Armory Newsletter*, November 2013.

Other

Naval History and Heritage Command. "Seabee History: Formation of the Seabees and World War II." https://www.history.navy.mil/research/library/online-reading-room/title-list-alphabetically/s/seabee-history0/world-war-ii.html.

CHAPTER 5. THE PT BOAT TRAINING CENTER AT MELVILLE

Books

Breuer, William. *Devil Boats: The PT War Against Japan*. Novato, CA: Presidio Press, 1987.

Bulkley, Robert J., Jr. *At Close Quarters, PT Boats in the United States Navy*. Washington, D.C.: GPO, 1962.

Chun, Victor. *American PT Boats in World War II*. Atglen, PA: Schiffer Publishing, 1997.

Donovan, Robert. *PT-109*. New York: McGraw Hill, 1961.

Friedman, Norman. *US Small Combatants*. Annapolis, MD: Naval Institute Press, 1987.

Jones, Charles B. *MTBSTC, Motor Torpedo Boat Squadrons Training Center*. Ann Arbor, MI: Nimble Books, 2011.

Tredinnick, Frank A., Jr., and Harrison L. Bennett. *An Administrative History of PTs in World War II*. Washington, D.C.: GPO, 1946.

Original Sources

Archival and Photographic Files. PT Boats Incorporated. National PT Boat Museum at Battleship Cove. Fall River, MA.

Evening Bulletin (Newport, RI). "PT Boat Crews Learned to Fight at Melville Base." November 7, 1945.

MTBSTC Files. MS Col. 18, folders 1–3. Naval War College Archives and Historic Collections. Newport, RI.

Newport Mercury. "Melville PT Base Ends Colorful Career." November 9, 1945.

———. "Ship Accidentally Torpedoed in Bay." April 17, 1942.

Other

U.S. Navy PT Boats of World War II. "MTB Training Center Melville Year One." http://pt-king.gdinc.com/Melville1.html.

CHAPTER 6. THE GROWTH OF NAVAL ACTIVITY AND ITS EFFECT ON AQUIDNECK ISLAND

Books

Office of Public Relations, Navy Department. *Report on the Navy and the War.* Part 1. Washington, D.C.: GPO, 1943.

U.S. Navy Department. *Dictionary of American Naval Fighting Ships.* Vol. 2. Washington, D.C.: GPO, 1963.

Williams, Glenn. *USS Constellation: A Short History of the Last All-Sail Warship Built by the U.S. Navy.* Virginia Beach, VA: Donning Company, 2000.

Periodicals

Panaggio, Leonard. "Grist Mill." *Newport Daily News,* August 13 and 15, 2011.

Original Sources

Command History—U.S. Naval Training Station/U.S. Naval Station, Newport, Rhode Island, 1639 Through 1958. Naval War College, Newport, RI.

Federal Owned Real Estate—Navy Department: Rhode Island: General Cession of Jurisdiction. Naval War College, Newport, RI.

Records of Naval Districts and Shore Establishments. Records of the Naval Training Station, Newport, Rhode Island. General Correspondence 1921–1939, National Archives RG 181, National Archives.

Records of Naval Districts and Shore Establishments. Records of the Naval Training Station, Newport, Rhode Island. Pre-Commissioning Training Files, 1944-46, National Archives RG 181, National Archives.

Records of the Bureau of Yards and Docks. Naval Property Case Files, Boxes 1127-1134, National Archives RG 71, National Archives.

Other

United States Atlantic Fleet, Confidential Memorandum, January 29, 1942. Newport, RI. www.history.navy.mil (search for "United States Atlantic Fleet Organization 1942").

CHAPTER 7. LIBERTY SHIPS AND MORE: CIVILIAN WORKERS AND MANUFACTURERS BOLSTER THE WAR EFFORT

The author thanks Christian McBurnery for providing some material for this chapter.

Books

Andresen, Robert L. *Providence Shipyard: Walsh-Kaiser Company, Inc., Shipbuilding Division, Providence, R.I., 1943–1945*. Providence, RI: Bank Lithograph Company, 1945.

Bunker, John G. *Liberty Ships. The Ugly Ducklings of World War II*. Annapolis, MD: Naval Institute Press, 1972.

Klein, Maury. *A Call to Arms, Mobilizing America for World War II*. New York: Bloomsbury Press, 2013.

100 Fighting Ships Built During World War II by Herreshoff. Bristol, RI: Herreshoff Manufacturing Company, 1945.

Periodicals

Chiappinelli, S. Robert, "The War Years: Everyone Pitches In—Three Years, 63 Ships at Field's Point." *Providence Journal*, June 28, 1999.

MacKay, Scott, and Jody McPhillips. "War Puts R.I. Back to Work, Supplying Troops." *Providence Journal*, June 27, 1999.

Morgan, Thomas J. "Book Records Liberty Ship History." *Providence Journal*, September 26, 2010.

———. "Shipyard Launched Liberty Ships During World War II." *Providence Journal*, September 26, 2010.

Rice, Chester A. "Boat Building in Greenwich Cove." *East Greenwich Packet* 6, no.1 (February 1982): 63.

Original Sources

Hearings Before the Subcommittee on Production in Shipbuilding Plants of the Committee on the Merchant Marine and Fisheries. 78th Cong. (March 29, 30, 31, April 4, 5, 26, and 27, 1944).

Other

For a list of ships constructed at each shipyard, see www.shipbuildinghistory.com/history/shipyards.

CHAPTER 8. WOMEN AT WORK OUTSIDE THE HOME

Books

Schroder, Walter K., and Gloria A. Emma. *Davisville and the Seabees*. Charleston, SC: Arcadia Publishing, 1999.

Periodicals

Lancaster, Jane, ed. "'I Go into Detail Mostly on Account of Posterity': Extracts from the World War II Diary of Helen Clarke Grimes." *Rhode Island History* 63, no. 1 (Winter/Spring 2005): 3–24.

MacKay, Scott. "Answering the Call—Old Barriers Fell as WWII Drafted Women into the Workplace." *Providence Journal*, March 26, 2000.

Morgan, Tom. "'Rosie the Riveter' Remembers." *Providence Journal*, September 26, 2010.

Original Sources

Aschman, Elisabeth Kellogg Sheldon. Interview by Christian McBurney. May 28, 2016.

Aukerman, Louise. Interview by Erika Hodges. Oral History of Rhode Island Women During World War II Written by Students in the Honors English Program at South Kingstown High School, 1988–89.

Chatalian, Mildred. Interview by Paul Rogers. Oral History of Rhode Island Women During World War II Written by Students in the Honors English Program at South Kingstown High School, 1988–89.

Craig, Naomi. Interview by Aileen Keenan. Oral History of Rhode Island Women During World War II Written by Students in the Honors English Program at South Kingstown High School, 1988–89.

MacDonald, Louise Roberts Sheldon. E-mail to Christian McBurney. April 18, 2016.

O'Grady, Katherine. Interview by Kathy O'Grady. Oral History of Rhode Island Women During World War II Written by Students in the Honors English Program at South Kingstown High School, 1988–89.

CHAPTER 9. THE RISE OF DAY NURSERIES IN PROVIDENCE

Original Sources

Dodd, W. Earl, ed. *Resolutions and Ordinances of the City Council of the City of Providence with Reports and Finished Business in the City Council, January 1942 to January 1943.* Providence, RI: Oxford Press, 1943.

Providence Day Nursery Association. *Annual Report of Nickerson Settlement House and School of Home Training.* Providence, RI: 1945.

Periodicals

Evening Bulletin (Providence, RI). "Day Nursery for Youngster of War-Working Parents." September 24, 1942.

Hull, George C. "Day Nursery Bright Place in World Clouded by War." *Providence Sunday Journal*, February 7, 1943.

Providence Journal. "Day Nurseries Saved in State." October 1, 1943.

———. "New Day Nursery to Start Monday." February 20, 1943.

Yardam. "Schools for Children of Working Mothers Opened." September 22, 1943.

———. "Woman Welder Becomes 150,000th Blue Cross Member." October 20, 1943.

CHAPTER 10. THE U.S. ARMY HANDLES COASTAL DEFENSE

Historical research on this topic is dominated by Walter K. Schroder's excellent *Defenses of Narragansett Bay in World War II.* Providence: Rhode Island Publications Society, 1980.

Books

Berhow, Mark, ed. *American Seacoast Defenses: A Reference Guide.* 2nd ed. Bel Air, MD: CDSG Press, 2004.

Downie, Robert. *Block Island—The Land.* Block Island, RI: Book Nook Press, 2001.

Duchesneau, John, and Kathleen Troost-Cramer. *Fort Adams: A History.* Charleston, SC: The History Press, 2014.

Eno, Paul F., and Glenn V. Laxton. *Rhode Island: A Genial History.* Woonsocket: New River Press, 2005.

Ignasher, Jim. *Rhode Island Disasters: Tales of Tragedy by Air, Sea and Rail.* Charleston, SC: The History Press, 2010.

Original Sources

History of the Northeastern Sector, Eastern Defense Command. 3 vols. Silver Spring, MD: War Department, 1945.

Kierstead, Matthew A. National Register of Historic Places Nomination Hillsgrove State Airport Historic District, Warwick, Kent County, Rhode Island. National Register No. 83000175, 2009.

CHAPTER 11. THE TOP-SECRET PRISONER-OF-WAR CAMP AT FORT KEARNEY IN NARRAGANSETT

Books

Andersch, Alfred. *My Disappearance in Providence and Other Stories.* Garden City, NY: Doubleday, 1977.

Gansberg, Judith M. *Stalag, U.S.A.: The Remarkable Story of German POWs in America.* New York: Crowell, 1977.

Horton, Aaron D. *German POWs, Der Ruf, and the Genesis of Group 47: The Political Journey of Alfred Andersch and Hans Werner Richter*. Lanham, MD: Farleigh Dickinson University Press, 2014.

Robin, Rob. *The Barbed Wire College, Reeducating German POWs in the United States During World War II*. Princeton, NJ: Princeton University Press, 1995.

Periodicals

Stets, Dan. "'The Spirit of Kearney.'" *Providence Sunday Journal*, July 18, 1982.

Various editions of *Der Ruf*, March 6, 1945, to April 1, 1946.

Original Sources

Edward Davison Papers, YCAL MSS 787, Series I: Military Files, Yale University Library, New Haven, CT.

Hazard, Michael. E-mails to Brian L. Wallin, 2015.

Records of the Office of the Provost Marshal General, 1920–1975, RG 389, National Archives, Building 2, College Park, MD.

Ross, Neil. E-mails to Christian McBurney, 2015.

Schroder, Walter K. Files, Rhode Island Historical Society (including copies of contemporary *Providence Journal* and other newspaper articles).

Wright, Charles "Ted." Interview by Christian McBurney, 2015.

Other

The authors thank Joachim Metzner of Wolfsburg, Germany, for sharing with them his treasure-trove of materials relating to the time spent by his father, Paul Metzner, as a POW at Fort Kearney.

CHAPTER 12. THE SPECIAL PRISONER-OF-WAR CAMPS AT FORTS GETTY AND WETHERILL IN JAMESTOWN

The same sources used for chapter 11 were used for this one, with the following additions.

Periodicals

Amarillo (TX) *Daily News*, June 21, 1946.

Campbell, Geoff. "POW Camps Little-Known Part of Island Legacy." *Jamestown Press*, August 5, 2010.

Fitchburg (MA) *Sentinel*, April 29, 1948.

Newport Mercury, September 28, 1945; February 1 and 15, 1946; and October 11, 1946.

Smith, T.V. "Behind the Barbed Wire." *Saturday Review of Literature*, May 4, 1946.

Original Sources

Härtle, Heinz. Letter to Edward Elliot, April 25, 1946. Martha Hartman Collection. Transcribed by Sam Elliot.

Ruchti, James R. Interview. January 13, 1997. Franklin D. Schurz Library, Indiana University. https://www.iusb.edu/library/about/collection/archives/ruchti/pow.php.

CHAPTER 13. THE BATTLE OF POINT JUDITH AND THE SINKINGS OF *BLACK POINT* AND *U-853*

Books

Downie, Robert. *Block Island—The Land*. Block Island, RI: Book Nook Press, 1999.

Guldemond, Cindy Follett. *Salt of the Sea: Stories Told by the Fishermen of Point Judith*. North Stonington, CT: Fowler Road Press, 2012.

Kemp, Paul. *U-Boats Destroyed: German Submarine Losses in the World Wars*. Annapolis, MD: Naval Institute Press, 1997.

Offley, Ed. *The Burning Shore, How Hitler's U-Boats Brought War to America*. New York: Basic Books, 2014.

Palmer, Captain Bill. *The Last Battle of the Atlantic: The Sinking of the* U-853. Wallingford, CT: Thunderfish Video and Publications, 2012.

Puelo, Stephen. *The True World War II Story of the USS* Eagle 56. Guildford, CT: Lyons Press, 2005.

Periodicals

Arnold, David. "The Final Hours of the *U-853*." *Boston Globe*, May 5, 1985.

Arsenault, Mark. "The Night World War II Came to R.I." *Providence Journal*, May 6, 1998.

Boston Globe. "39 Saved, One Missing after Sub Scores Three Hits Close Off L.I. Shore." January 15, 1942.

Carbone, Gerald M. "'They Were All Somebody's Sons.'" *Providence Journal*, May 6, 1995.

Carr, Robert, B. "U-Boat, Sunk Off Block Island, Center of Row." *Boston Globe*, November 6, 1960.

Lynch, Adam. "Kill and Be Killed? The *U-853* Mystery." *Naval History Magazine* 22, no. 3 (June 2008).

Newport Daily News. "U-Boat Sunk 23 Years Ago Still on Bottom," November 19, 1968.

———. October 25, 1960; January 17, 21 and 31, 1961; February 23, 1961; and May 2, 1961.

Reach, Thomas, and Elliot Subervi. "The Twisted Fate of *U-853*." *Skin Diver*, March 1974.

Tollaksen, D. M. "Last Chapter for *U-853*." *U.S. Naval Institute Proceedings* 86, no. 12 (December 1960): 82–89.

Original Sources

Albin, G.W. Jr. Letter to Chaplain J.P. Gallagher, undated. *U-853* File, Naval War College Archives.

Coward, Lieutenant Barbara. Memorandum dated May 14, 1945. *U-853* file, UD-09D 19, No. 26870453, U.S. Department of Navy files, National Archives, Silver Spring, MD.

Other

DiCarpio, Ralph. "The Battle of Point Judith." Destroyer Escort Sailors Association. http://www.desausa.org/Stories/battle_of_point_judith_2.htm.

World Public Library. "German Submarine *U-853*." www.worldlibrary.org/articles/German_submarine_U-853.

Chapter 14. Reflection, Relief and Rowdiness: Rhode Islanders React to the End of World War II

Books

Verria, Lawrence, and George Galdorisi. *The Kissing Sailor: The Mystery Behind the Photo that Ended World War II*. Annapolis, MD: Naval Institute Press, 2012.

Periodicals

Gudrais, Elizabeth. "They Called It Victory Day." *Providence Journal*, August 8, 2005.

Newpoer Navalog. "Rededication to the Job, Smashing Japan, is NTS Reaction to V-E." May 12, 1945.

Providence Journal. "Calm Observance of V-E Day Noted." May 9, 1945.

————. "City Lets Loose in Carnival Eclipsing that of Nov. 11, '18." August 15, 1945.

————. "Cranston Stages Gala Observance." August 15, 1945.

————. "East Providence Shouts for Joy." August 15, 1945.

————. "Toast to Five Soldier Sons." May 9, 1945.

————. "V-E Celebrations Close R.I. Plants." May 9, 1945.

Providence Sunday Journal. "A Generation Remembers." August 13, 1995.

Original Sources

"History of the WAVES, no. 62: Nellie Moore Rollins." Oral History Program, Naval War College, 1998.

Other

"Nurse Kissed in Iconic V-J Day Photo Dead at 92." CNN. http://www.cnn.com/2016/09/10/us/greta-friedman-iconic-kissing-vj-day-photo-obit-irpt/index.html.

"V-J Day: A War, a Kiss, a Mystery." CNN. http://www.cnn.com/2015/08/14/us/vj-day-kissing-sailor/index.html.

"V-J Day in Times Square." *Wikipedia*. https://en.wikipedia.org/wiki/V-J_Day_in_Times_Square.

Index

A

Administration School 128
Advance Base Depot 9, 31, 34, 35, 48,
      49, 50, 97, 103, 162
Advance Base Proving Ground 9, 50, 103
Africa 38, 51, 110, 111, 129, 133, 142
African Americans (in the military and
      civilian workforce) 29, 75, 90,
      94, 131
Aircraft Anti-Submarine Development
      Detachment 42
Albin, George Waugh, Jr. (Lieutenant
      Commander) 146
Alice Mill 80
Allen Harbor 50, 103
Allen, William Slater 31
American Federation of Labor 84, 87
Amore, Rose 93, 97
Anchorage Incorporated 80
Andersch, Alfred 116, 122, 123, 125
Anderson Sheet Metal Co. 51
Anti-Aircraft Training Center 62, 69,
      107, 161
Aquidneck Island, Rhode Island 58,
      62, 67–73, 76, 161
Argentia, Newfoundland, Canada 38

Asplund, Oswald Eugene, Jr. (Ensign) 40
Aukerman, Louise 91
Auxiliary Attack Cargo Ships (AKAs) 85

B

Base Realignment and Closure (BRAC)
      76
Battle of Point Judith 142–148, 150
Beach, Edward L. (Captain) 25
Beavertail Point, Rhode Island 42, 44,
      107, 108
Biltmore Hotel 79
Bingham, William (Lieutenant Colonel)
      123
Black Point 11, 137, 141, 142, 150
Blackstone Valley, Rhode Island 78,
      79, 91
Blair, Alcina (Lopes) 132
blimps 145, 146
Block Island, Rhode Island 17, 41, 57,
      105, 108, 137, 138, 141, 143
Block Island Sound 40, 96
Bockelman, Edwin J.R. 146, 148
Boston, Massachusetts 32, 104, 142,
      145, 146, 148
Bradley Field 109
Braine, Clinton E. (Commodore) 152

Brandenberger, Otto 51
Brenton Point, Rhode Island 104
Bristol, Rhode Island 11, 79, 80
Browe, Jerry 72
Brown & Sharpe 79, 87, 91, 92, 93, 95
Bryan, Blackshear M. (General) 119
Burbine, Joe 142
Bureau of Yards and Docks 34, 47, 70
Bush, George H.W. (President) 11, 44, 46

C

Camp Endicott 47, 48, 49, 77. *See also* Naval
        Construction Training Center
Camp Thomas 50
Cape Cod, Massachusetts 35, 44, 90, 142
Carbone, Gerald M. 40
Catholicism 75
Central Falls, Rhode Island 152
Central Torpedo Office 20
Charlestown, RI 9, 31, 44, 46. *See
        also* Naval Auxiliary Air Facility
        Charlestown
Chase, Richard (Captain) 121
Chatalian, Mildred 92
Chopmist Hill 111
Christie, Ralph (Admiral) 25
Christman, Delores 132
Clary, David 147
Coasters Harbor Island, Rhode Island
        13, 65, 72
Coddington Cove, Rhode Island 20, 30
Coddington Point, Rhode Island 19,
        53, 65, 68, 74
Coleman Construction 59
Conanicut Island. *See* Jamestown
Conanicut Island, Rhode Island 21,
        66, 72, 107, 125, 128
Correira, Sergio 152
Council of Defense (RI) 14, 17
Craig, Naomi 90
Cranston Arms Company Inc. 79
Cranston, Rhode Island 79, 83, 152
Cumberland, Rhode Island 92

D

Davison, Edward (Lieutenant Colonel)
        113, 127, 134
Davisville, Rhode Island 9, 16, 31, 34,
        44, 47, 48, 50, 66, 67, 77, 97,
        103, 152, 162
Davol Corporation 79
day nurseries 99, 101, 102
Deisting, Helga 140
Dejongh, Peter 51
Delaney, Jack 46
Demurs, Joseph 18
Der Ruf 117, 118, 119, 124
Destroyer Escort Historical Museum
        150
diPretoro, Jack 23
Doggett, William 17
Dönitz, Karl (Admiral) 140
Dumplings, the 41
Dunes Club 96
Dutch Island, Rhode Island 105

E

Eastern Sea Frontier 138, 142, 146
East Greenwich, Rhode Island 11, 75,
        80, 107
East Providence, Rhode Island 153
Edison, Charles (Secretary of the Navy) 31
Ehrmann, Dr. Henry 131
Eisenstaedt, Alfred 153
Endicott Fort 105, 114

F

Fall River, Massachusetts 7, 62, 64, 67
Federal Bureau of Investigation (FBI)
        15, 18, 44, 132
Federal Products Company 79
Field's Point, Rhode Island 11, 27, 82,
        87, 88, 103
Fireside Builders Products Corporation 79
First Naval District 142
First Service Command 123
Fonda, Henry 44
Fort Adams 11, 15, 23, 30, 104, 108, 121

Fort Burnside 107
Fort Church 105, 108
Fort Devens (MA) 109, 133
Fort Eustis (VA) 134
Fort Getty 107, 108, 127–135
Fort Greble 105
Fort Greene 105, 108, 142
Fort Kearney 96, 105, 107, 108,
     113–125, 127, 130
Fort Varnum 107
Fort Wetherill 108, 127–135, 128, 129,
     131, 135
Friedman, Greta 155
Friendly, Fred 33
Frömsdorf, Helmut (Captain) 139–141,
     143, 144, 150

G

Galdorisi, George 154
Gallo, Selma 93
Gannon, James (Ensign) 46
Gannon, Robert 28
Gariepy, Del 80
Gauthier, Jacqueline 153
Gazda, Antoine 79
George A. Fuller Company 32, 51, 53
German prisoners-of-war 11, 15,
     113–135, 135
Germany
   military forces 67, 80, 83, 137–141,
        146, 148, 151
   postwar 124, 127, 133, 135, 149
Gilbane Building Company 32, 59
Goat Island, Rhode Island 13, 19, 27,
     29, 59, 65, 70, 74, 78, 107
Gorham Manufacturing Company 79,
     87, 152
Gould Island, Rhode Island 19, 23, 26,
     30, 62, 65, 71, 76
Government Pier 27
Great Britain 26, 85
Great Depression 9, 24, 89
Green, Theodore Francis (Senator) 28, 66
Grimes, Helen Clark 13, 95
Groton, Connecticut 44, 110

Group of 47 125
Grove Point, Rhode Island 143

H

Haffenreffer, Carl W. 80
Haines, Ralph E. (General) 17
Hallstein, Dr. Walter 130, 135
Halsband, Shirley 91
Hansen, Nicholas 18
Harbor Defenses of Narragansett Bay
     17, 104, 108
Harris and Parsons 80
Hartford, CT 109
Härtle, Heinz 133
Hazard, C. Michael 123
Hepburn Board 31
Herreshoff Manufacturing Company
     7, 80
Herreshoff, Rebecca Chase 97
Hetzfuss, Gerhard 132
Hillsgrove Army Airfield 109
Hitler, Adolf 113, 117, 119, 131, 139
Hitler, William Patrick 44
Hocke, Dr. Gustav R. 117, 120
Hoffmann, Herbert 147
Hog Island, Rhode Island 23
Homberger, Kenneth 144
Hope Island, Rhode Island 21, 33, 71
Hughes, Eileen 96
H.V. Collins 59

I

Iafrate, Frank 49
Ignasher, Jim 40
Imperial Knife Company 79
Ingersoll, Royal E. (Admiral) 75
Iselin, Lewis (Lieutenant Commander)
     143, 145, 150
Island Cemetery 42, 139, 148, 150

J

Jamestown Bridge 13, 96
Jamestown, Rhode Island 11, 15, 21,
     23, 27, 41, 42, 46, 63, 73, 75,
     77, 104, 108, 114, 120, 122,
     128, 132, 133, 135
Japan
   military forces 13, 24, 26, 31, 38, 46, 47,
     56, 68, 83, 85, 89, 111, 121, 152
Jones, Howard Mumford 120
Judaism 50, 75, 115, 117, 119

K

Kaiser, Henry J. 84, 100
Kalbfus, Edward C. (Admiral) 58, 66, 138
Kamen 142
Kearny, Phillip (General) 114
Kennedy, John F. (President) 11, 56, 57
Keough, Francis P. (Most Reverent) 151
Keys, Eleanor 94, 97
King, Ernest (Admiral) 26
Kingston, Rhode Island 18, 115
Klein, Maury 28
Knox, Frank (Secretary of the Navy)
     48, 58, 61, 66
Kolster, Kenneth K. 131
Kuhnke, Günther 140, 148
Kunzig, Robert L. (Captain) 115, 116,
     118, 121

L

Lakehurst, New Jersey 145
Lamoureaux, A.J. (Lieutenant Colonel) 123
Liberty ships 11, 31, 49, 82, 83, 85,
     93, 95
Liberty Tool & Gauge Company 79
Little Compton, Rhode Island 11, 77,
     105, 138
Locke, Howard 142
Lockwood, Charles (Admiral) 26
Long Island, New York 16, 32, 35, 37, 96

M

Macdonald, Jack 84
MAD (Magnetic Anomaly Detection)
     42, 140, 145
Manville-Jenckes Mill 79
Maritime Commission 82, 84
Martha's Vineyard, Massachusetts 37, 44
Mason, Burton 148, 149
Massachusetts 41, 44, 58, 59, 83, 105, 123
McFall, A.C. (Commander) 34
McGrath, J. Howard (Governor) 14,
     16, 87, 100, 151
McKnight, Maxwell (Major) 113
Mellor, Robert 49
Melville, Rhode Island 9, 22, 53,
     55–65, 67, 103, 108, 138, 144
Mendonsa, George 153, 155
Metzner, Joachim 177
Middletown, Rhode Island 70, 138, 153
Miller, Virginia 91
Miner, Mary 23
Montauk Point, New York 37
Moran, Phil 153
Moreell, Ben (Admiral) 34, 47, 49
Motor Torpedo Boat Repair Training
     Unit 61, 162
Motor Torpedo Boat Squadrons
     Training Center 53, 55–64, 161
Mount Hope Bridge 56, 61, 73
Mulligan, Sean Paul 35, 38

N

Nantucket Island, Massachusetts 37,
     44, 138
Narragansett Bay, Rhode Island 11,
     13, 57–67, 65, 78, 105, 114,
     121, 128, 137, 139, 141
Narragansett, Rhode Island 11, 77,
     105, 113, 123, 138
National Catholic Community Service 75
National Guard 16, 32, 104, 108
National Jewish Welfare Board 75
National PT Boat Museum 64
Naval Aircraft Rework Facility 42

Naval Air Station Lakehurst (NAS Lakehurst) 145
Naval Air Station Quonset Point (NAS Quonset Point) 9, 16, 22, 31–44, 53, 64, 66, 77, 96, 103, 138, 140, 162
Naval Air Station (South Weymouth) 140
Naval Auxiliary Air Facility Charlestown (NAAF Charlestown) 9, 44–46, 77
Naval Auxiliary Air Facility Westerly (NAAF Westerly) 9, 31, 44, 46, 77, 160
Naval Communication Station Newport 70
Naval Construction Training Center 9, 48, 67, 103, 162. *See also* Camp Endicott
Naval Fuel Depot 59, 61, 64, 71, 77, 161
Naval Hospital 65, 90, 138, 161
Naval Net Depot 61, 64, 67, 108
Naval Operating Base Newport (NOB Newport) 58, 66, 161
Naval Reserve 43, 57, 66, 90
Naval Rifle Range 70
Naval Supply Depot 67, 68, 162
Naval Torpedo Station 9, 13, 18–30, 71, 78, 91, 94, 97, 103, 161
Naval Training School 43
Naval Training Station 9, 13, 53, 65, 67–69, 78, 103, 161
Naval Underwater Systems Center 30
Naval War College 65, 66, 74, 78, 150, 155, 161
Naval War College Museum 30, 146
Navy Department 32, 65, 76
Nazis and Nazism 113, 115, 117, 119, 121, 124, 127, 129, 132, 135, 141, 151
neutrality patrols 32
New Bedford, Massachusetts 44, 67, 138
New England 9, 32, 40, 65, 87, 123, 132, 137
New London, Connecticut 148
Newport Harbor 19

Newport Housing Authority 73
Newport Naval Base 55, 58, 148
Newport, Rhode Island 19–30, 32, 37, 42, 53, 58, 61, 62, 65–75, 82, 91, 94, 104, 107, 122, 123, 128, 155, 161
New York, New Haven and Hartford Railroad 15, 70, 105
New York, New York 15, 32, 47, 59, 84, 117, 131, 133, 135, 138, 142, 146, 153
Nickerson Settlement House 102
Night Attack and Combat Training Unit-Atlantic 46
night fighting 38, 46
Nixon, Richard M. (President) 11
Nonquit Pond 73
Norness 137
North Kingstown, Rhode Island 40, 47
North Providence, Rhode Island 49

O

Oerlikon-Gazda antiaircraft gun 11, 79, 91
Office of the Provost Marshal 133
O'Grady, Katherine 94
O'Kane, Richard 24
Old Colony Railroad 76
Olsen, Robert (Captain) 148
Otis Field (NAAF Otis) 44

P

Packard Engines 59, 61
Pantex Pressing Machine Company 79
Pawtucket, Rhode Island 11, 67, 79, 93, 152, 153
Pearl Harbor 13, 18, 26, 28, 47, 57, 60, 68, 82, 89, 105, 119
Pennington, Joseph 17
Perkins & Vaughan 80
Pestalozzi, Robert (Lieutenant) 119
Point Judith. *See* Battle of Point Judith
Point Judith Coast Guard Station 142
Point Judith, Rhode Island 11, 105, 137, 138, 142

Police School 128, 131
pontoons 9, 47, 50, 79
Portsmouth, Rhode Island 55, 73
Price's Neck, Rhode Island 62, 69, 107
Prior, Charles E. (Captain) 141
Providence, Rhode Island 11, 14, 15, 18, 23, 27, 32, 46, 52, 59, 62, 67, 79, 82–88, 92, 93, 95, 102, 103, 151, 153
Providence Shipyard 82–88, 92, 95
Prudence Island, Rhode Island 21, 71
PT boats 9, 19, 22, 55–64, 64, 80, 138
PT Boats Inc. 55, 64

Q

Queen Mary 111, 139
Quonset hut 9, 47, 50, 52, 53, 59, 64, 68, 71, 77
Quonset Point, Rhode Island 9, 16, 31–44, 53, 96, 111, 141, 142. *See also* Naval Air Station Quonset Point

R

radar 9, 42, 46, 59, 85, 105, 107, 138, 140
Rheem Manufacturing Company 82, 84
Rhode Island Sound 32, 105, 137, 139, 141, 142
Richmond, Rhode Island 92
Richter, Hans Werner 121, 125
Roberts, Dennis J. (Mayor) 88
Robinson House 76
Rogers High School 28
Rogers, William 43
Rollins, Nellie Moore 152
Romano Vineyard 32
Roosevelt, Franklin D. (President) 11, 13, 18, 31, 65, 75, 87, 94, 151
Rose Island, Rhode Island 65, 72
Ross, Neil 123
Royal Navy 41, 85
Ruchti, James 130
Rust, Joseph Clyde (Ensign) 40

S

sabotage 14, 17, 103
Sachuest Point, Rhode Island 70, 138
Sakonnett Point, Rhode Island 105
Sakonnett River 42
Salvation Army 75, 102
Sandwich, Massachusetts 44
Sandy Point, Rhode Island 141
Saunderstown, Rhode Island 18, 96, 105, 108, 113, 123
Sawmill Pond 40
Scheibl, Fred 28
Schönstedt, Walter (Captain) 119
Schroder, Walter K. 122, 125, 175
Scituate, Rhode Island 17, 111
Seabees 9, 47, 49, 51, 75, 77, 94, 97
Sheffield, George 17
Sheldon, Elisabeth 18
Sheldon, Louise 96
Sheldon, Margaret Chase 96
Shippee, Clair 92
Smith, Alpheus W. (Lieutenant Colonel) 128, 134
Smith, T.V. 130
Sommers, Helmut (Captain) 141
South Ferry, Rhode Island 113, 125
South Weymouth, Massachusetts 140
Soviet Union 80, 125, 133
Specht, William C. (Lieutenant Commander) 59, 60, 62
Special Projects Division 113, 116, 121, 127, 129
Spraycliff Observatory 42, 46
Stokes, Ruth Barclay 29, 95
Straiten, Grace 94
Strunz, Henry 18
submarine net (antisubmarine net) 61, 71, 108, 161
submarines 9, 11, 20–25, 30, 46, 72, 96, 105, 108, 137–150. *See also* U-boats

T

Taft-Pierce Manufacturing Company 79
Taylor, Erich O'D. 17
Taylor, William E.G. (Commander) 46
Theodore Francis Green Memorial State Airport 15, 109. *See also* Hillsgrove Army Airfield
Tiverton, Rhode Island 73
Tollaksen, Leslie B. (Lieutenant Commander) 142
torpedoes 9, 13, 30, 37, 39, 57, 63, 71, 79, 91, 137, 140, 141, 144
Torpedo Station. *See* Naval Torpedo Station
Training Station. *See* Naval Training Station
Truman, Harry S. (Vice President and President) 87, 151
Trumbull Field 110

U

U-boats 9, 11, 23, 35, 37, 108, 111, 137–150
 U-123 137
 U-550 138
 U-853 11, 137, 139, 140, 143, 145, 147, 150
unions 28, 29, 79, 84, 92
Universal Winding Company 79
U.S. Army 11, 17, 18, 36, 61, 72, 89, 91, 93, 103, 107, 109, 114, 119, 127, 130
U.S. Army aircraft
 P-40 Warhawks 38, 110
 P-47 Thunderbolts 110
U.S. Army School Center 128
U.S. Army units
 10th Coast Artillery Regiment 104
 22nd Quartermaster Regiment 104
 33rd Pursuit Squadron 38
 57th Fighter Group 38
 132nd Engineer Battalion 104
 152nd Observation Squadron 108

181st Infantry Regiment 104
207th Coast Artillery Regiment 104, 107
211th Field Artillery Battalion 104
243rd Coast Artillery Regiment 104, 105
325th Fighter Group 109
352nd Fighter Group 110
U.S. Coast Guard 17, 18, 21, 76, 90, 96, 103, 138, 142
U.S. Coast Guard vessels
 USS *Moberly* 142, 144, 146
U.S. Marine Corps 79, 83, 84, 89, 91, 103, 148, 161, 162
U.S. Merchant Marine 83, 89
U.S. Navy vessels
 PT-59 63
 PT-109 56
 PT-200 64
 USS *Amick* 142
 USS *Atherton* 142, 144
 USS *Augusta* 15, 38, 68, 75
 USS *Block Island* 37
 USS *Cachalot* 23
 USS *Capella* 63
 USS *Columbus* 68
 USS *Constellation* 75, 162
 USS *Eagle Boat* 56 140
 USS *Ellyson* 138
 USS *Enterprise* 26
 USS *Franklin* 68
 USS *Hornet* 26
 USS *Muskeogen* 140
 USS *Penguin* 146
 USS *Ranger* 37, 39, 41
 USS *San Jacinto* 45
 USS *Santa Fe* 69
USO 61, 75, 96
U.S. Rubber Company 79

V

Vanderbilt, William H. III (Governor) 66
V-E Day 152
Verria, Lawrence 154
Vickery, Howard (Admiral) 82

Vinz, Curt 117
V-J Day 152, 153, 155

W

Wakefield, Rhode Island 40, 49, 123
Walsh Company 84
Walsh-Kaiser Company Inc. 82, 84, 85, 88
Walsh-Kaiser Shipyard 11, 18, 27, 82–88, 88, 95, 103. *See also* Providence Shipyard
Walsh, Thomas J. 84
Warden's Pond 40
War Department 11, 65, 115, 117, 128
Warfield, Thomas (Commander) 62
Warren Boat Yard 80
Warren, Rhode Island 11, 73, 80, 152
War Shipping Administration 83
Warwick, Rhode Island 11, 108
Watch Hill, Rhode Island 11, 105
Watertown, Massachusetts 105
Weiss, Gerhard 119, 122
West Davisville, Rhode Island 52, 53
Westerly Airport 44. *See also* Naval Auxiliary Air Facility Westerly
Westerly, Rhode Island 9, 31, 44, 77, 107
West Warwick, Rhode Island 18
Weymouth, Massachusetts 141
Wheeler, Henry C. 66
Wickford, Rhode Island 11, 80
Wilimzig, Imfried 119
Wischnewski, Franz 115, 122
women
   in defense factories 11, 18, 29, 77, 87, 91–95, 100, 102
   in the military 19, 42, 90
women's military organizations
   CB-ettes Club 97
   Navy Nurse Corps 90
   SPARs (U.S. Coast Guard) 90
   WACs (Women's Army Corps) 90
   WAVES (Women Accepted for Volunteer Emergency Service, U.S. Navy Reserves) 42, 90, 152

Woonsocket, Rhode Island 11, 14, 67, 80, 103, 152
Works Progress Administration 99
World War I 15, 22, 57, 65, 109, 128
Wright, Charles "Ted" 123

Y

YMCA 23, 75
YWCA 75

Z

Zander, Wolf 129, 131, 134, 135

About the Authors

Each of the authors is also a contributing author to the Online Review of Rhode Island History at www.smallstatebighistory.com. To find articles by them, go to the website, click on the Archives tab and review the list of articles, or type in the author's name in the search box.

CHRISTIAN MCBURNEY, the primary editor of this book and the editor and publisher of the Online Review of Rhode Island History, has written seven books on Rhode Island and/or Revolutionary War history. For more information on his books go to www.christian.mcburney.com.

BRIAN L. WALLIN spent the first half of his career as a radio and television journalist for major stations in Connecticut, Massachusetts and Rhode Island and the second half working as a healthcare executive for hospital systems in Massachusetts and Rhode Island. In addition to being a frequent contributor to the Online Review of Rhode Island History, he is a trustee of the Varnum Continentals historic militia and the Varnum Armory Museum.

PATRICK T. CONLEY is president of the Rhode Island Heritage Hall of Fame, president of the Heritage Harbor Foundation, chairman of the Rhode Island Publications Society and currently serving as the first historian laureate of the State of Rhode Island. For more information on the twenty-nine books he has authored, as well as other Rhode Island history books, go to www. ripublications.org.

JOHN W. KENNEDY is a retired naval officer who for the last seven and a half years served as the director of education and community outreach for the Naval War College Museum at Newport. In that capacity, he ran the popular Eight Bells history lecture series. He retired in 2016.

MAUREEN A. TAYLOR is the author of sixteen books on family history and photography, as well as Rhode Island history. The *Wall Street Journal* called her "the nation's foremost photo detective." For more information on her books, go to www.maureentaylor.com.